D0780328

CALGARY PUBLIC LIBRARY

JUL     2011

# THE ART OF
# THE SWING

# THE ART OF
# THE SWING

Short Game Swing-Sequencing Secrets That
Will Improve Your Total Game in 30 Days

## Stan Utley

with Matthew Rudy

GOTHAM
BOOKS

GOTHAM BOOKS
Published by Penguin Group (USA) Inc.
375 Hudson Street, New York, New York 10014, U.S.A.
Penguin Group (Canada), 90 Eglinton Avenue East, Suite 700, Toronto, Ontario M4P 2Y3,
Canada (a division of Pearson Penguin Canada Inc.); Penguin Books Ltd, 80 Strand, London
WC2R 0RL, England; Penguin Ireland, 25 St Stephen's Green, Dublin 2, Ireland (a division
of Penguin Books Ltd); Penguin Group (Australia), 250 Camberwell Road, Camberwell,
Victoria 3124, Australia (a division of Pearson Australia Group Pty Ltd); Penguin Books
India Pvt Ltd, 11 Community Centre, Panchsheel Park, New Delhi—110 017, India;
Penguin Group (NZ), 67 Apollo Drive, Rosedale, Auckland 0632, New Zealand (a
division of Pearson New Zealand Ltd); Penguin Books (South Africa) (Pty) Ltd, 24 Sturdee
Avenue, Rosebank, Johannesburg 2196, South Africa

Penguin Books Ltd, Registered Offices: 80 Strand, London WC2R 0RL, England

Published by Gotham Books, a member of Penguin Group (USA) Inc.

First printing, May 2011

10 9 8 7 6 5 4 3 2 1

Copyright © 2011 by Stan Utley

All rights reserved

Gotham Books and the skyscraper logo are trademarks of Penguin Group (USA) Inc.

LIBRARY OF CONGRESS CATALOGING-IN-PUBLICATION DATA HAS BEEN
APPLIED FOR.

ISBN 978-1-592-40627-2

Printed in the United States of America

Set in Berling LT Std

Designed by Sabrina Bowers

Without limiting the rights under copyright reserved above, no part of this publication may
be reproduced, stored in or introduced into a retrieval system, or transmitted, in any form,
or by any means (electronic, mechanical, photocopying, recording, or otherwise), without
the prior written permission of both the copyright owner and the above publisher of this
book.

The scanning, uploading, and distribution of this book via the Internet or via any other
means without the permission of the publisher is illegal and punishable by law. Please
purchase only authorized electronic editions, and do not participate in or encourage
electronic piracy of copyrighted materials. Your support of the author's rights is appreciated.

While the author has made every effort to provide accurate telephone numbers and Internet
addresses at the time of publication, neither the publisher nor the author assumes any
responsibility for errors, or for changes that occur after publication. Further, the publisher
does not have any control over and does not assume any responsibility for author or
third-party Web sites or their content.

**For Ruby and Frank**

# CONTENTS

How to Use This Book                                    ix

Foreword by Brandel Chamblee                            xi

Foreword by Tom Cisar                                   xv

Introduction                                            xvii

CHAPTER 1: FORM VS. SEQUENCE                            I

CHAPTER 2: MOVING ENERGY TO THE CLUBHEAD                27

CHAPTER 3: CONTROLLING THE CLUBFACE                     45

CHAPTER 4: SEQUENCING YOUR GAME                         59

CHAPTER 5: THE BOOK OF FEELS                            75

CHAPTER 6: ONE CLUB, FIVE SHOTS                         87

CHAPTER 7: THE FULL SWING                               105

CHAPTER 8: DIAGNOSING YOUR BALL FLIGHT                  117

CHAPTER 9: YOUR 30-DAY PRACTICE PLAN                    127

CHAPTER 10: SEQUENCING QUICK REFERENCE GUIDE            137

Acknowledgments                                         149

# HOW TO USE THIS BOOK

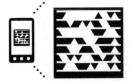

**Get the free mobile app at**
http://gettag.mobi

Throughout *The Art of the Swing*, you'll find a series of bar codes that look like the one printed here. These Microsoft Tags connect directly to a collection of my instruction videos designed to accompany the surrounding text in each chapter. To use the tag videos, you need a smartphone with a camera and the free Microsoft Tag app, which can be downloaded directly from the web browser on your phone at http://gettag.mobi, or through the Apple App Store. The app is free to download and use, and the videos connected to the tags in the book are exclusive to this book. The only way to get access to these comprehensive custom instruction videos is through the tag reader on your phone.

To use the app, simply click it from the menu on your phone, then aim the target in the viewfinder of your phone's camera so that the tag is centered on the screen. The video will pop up automatically. You don't even need to push a button.

If you don't have a smartphone or access to the tag reader, you can still enjoy *The Art of the Swing* the old-fashioned way—in your favorite chair or on a flight. The pages have been designed to flow like a conventional instruction book, with a layer of technology added on top.

I do hope you get the chance to take advantage of the video component we've paired with the printed material here. For a small-town Missouri boy, seeing the videos come to life right from the page is very, very cool—and one of the most helpful long-distance teaching tools I've seen.

I hope you enjoy it.

Stan Utley
February 18, 2011

# FOREWORD

## by Brandel Chamblee

The first time I ever saw the name Stan Utley was in 1983 at a college tournament in Monterrey, Mexico, of all places. I was playing for the University of Texas, and I had a pretty good day, shooting 65. I expected to be leading, and I was—by three or four. I went in and was enjoying my *tacos al carbón* for lunch when some of my friends came in to tell me that that some guy from Missouri had tied me.

Missouri?

I hadn't heard Stan's name before that, but it was one I'd become familiar with pretty fast. That year, because of the way Stan played, Missouri won their first conference title in forever—and that was no small accomplishment when you consider they were up against Oklahoma State and Colorado and Texas and Oklahoma. He ended up being named second-team All-American that year and the following one, his senior season. He and I played the same circuit of amateur events around the Midwest those years, and we also went out and tried to find our way on the PGA Tour at the same time, so it's not surprising that we became great friends. He's just a quality guy.

Then and now, when you played with Stan, you were never blown away by his athleticism or how long and straight he hit it. In fact, he had stretches where he really struggled with his accuracy. But he knew how to play golf.

Stan and I made our professional debuts at the same tournament, and we roomed together that week. I'll never forget it. The course was billed as the hardest in the world—7,200 yards of forced carry, water, and OB, back before Pete Dye brought those kinds of monstrosities into style. We played a practice round the day we arrived, and if he had added them up Stan might have shot 90. That night, over dinner, he was lamenting about how he had lost his game, and that he might be better off going home and working on it before he wasted any more money trying to be a pro.

The next day, I went out and shot 75—a good score on a cold, windy day. I came in and walked over to take a look at the board. Honestly, I was more worried that Stan had shot something really embarrassing or hadn't finished. I started at the bottom right, where the scores in the high 80s and 90s were. I kept scanning, looking for his name, and didn't see it. Out of the corner of my eye, way up in the top left, I could see one name three or four shots clear, but I didn't really pay attention to it. Sure enough, it was Stan's. He had shot a 68—which was more like a 62 under those conditions.

I found him in the clubhouse eating lunch, and I made a joke about him "losing his game." He smiled, and said he had found a go-to shot on the range—a fade—and he went around the whole day hitting that one shot. Stan would be the first to tell you he hasn't been blessed with tremendous speed or athletic ability. But he has incredible hand-eye coordination, and a disposition to not panic. Most people let ego strangle them. Stan stays within himself, and plays to his strengths.

The greatest of those strengths has always been hitting shots and making putts. It's been fascinating to watch him go through the process of analyzing the hows and whys of putting and short game, and to develop his talent for sharing what he knows with other players. On the tour, Stan starts from a position of authority. Regardless of how easy Tiger Woods has made it look for stretches of the last ten years, winning even once on tour is extremely difficult. When Stan had a putt to win an event, he made it. That matters.

On television, we love to talk about swing analysis and mechanics—the mathematics and angles of the golf swing. But most players—and teachers—take this game and make it more complicated than it needs to be. Genius is taking this game and making it simple. There's a reason Harvey Penick's *Little Red Book* is the most well-read instruction book there is. I have watched people get drawn to Stan during practice rounds, at the 19th hole, in the locker room, and at dinner for those same reasons. He has that rare talent of being able to simplify the game, and to share it in a way that makes sense to players at every level. It's no surprise to me that people want some of what he has—the quality of getting the ball in the hole.

There are some parts of a tour player's game that the average guy will never be able to replicate. It takes a special body type and an incredible dedication to practice to be able to generate the clubhead speed that most tour players achieve. But for all the parts that can be copied—putting, short game, good sequencing—Stan has created a blueprint here that the average player can actually follow and use to produce real results.

Listen to what he has to say—I know your game will improve.

BRANDEL CHAMBLEE
GOLF CHANNEL COMMENTATOR AND PGA TOUR WINNER
SCOTTSDALE, AZ
NOVEMBER 10, 2010

# FOREWORD

by Tom Cisar

first met Stan Utley about six years ago, when I was looking for some help with my short game. We have a mutual friend, and that friend helped me get onto Stan's busy teaching schedule at Grayhawk.

He didn't have any reason to give me special treatment, but after that first lesson, I learned an important thing about Stan Utley. Nothing is more important to him than helping someone. Whether he's working with one of his tour players, an avid amateur player like myself, or a complete beginner, his goal is to help and to help people enjoy this game.

That first lesson with Stan grew into a deep friendship. We have a lot of the same philosophies about how to treat our fellow men, and we're both men of faith. Our families have become close, and Stan has a couple of great kids that I've taken a shine to. They remind me of my own children, now grown.

Stan could have had any of the tour players he teaches introduce him to the readers of this book—and given how much prize money he's helped them earn, I'm sure they would have gladly done so. I'm extremely proud that he chose me, and I believe it's because he knows that the immense satisfaction he's helped me find in my own game is as valuable to me as any check a tour player could cash. I'm sixty-two years old, and with Stan's help, I've got a 1-handicap, and I'm playing as well or better as I did more than forty years ago as a college golfer at the University of Illinois-Chicago.

Stan is an incredible communicator, and he relates his message in such a clear way that anybody can take what he has to share and get better. Many teachers can give you something that will get you hitting good shots while they're standing there watching you, but then, when you're on your own, you lose your way. Stan helps you understand the way the club works, and how to manage your swing and your game on your own.

Shooting lower scores and enjoying the game more are obviously great, but for me, Stan's dedication and his connection to his students set him apart. He came out to play a round with me the last time he was in Chicago, and I was describing to him how my wife, Peggy, had just taken up the game. At the end of our round, he asked if it would be okay for him to take a look at Peggy's swing and give her a few tips. He spent the next hour with her, giving her an incredible foundation for her newborn golf game. By the end of the hour, more than forty people had gathered to watch the lesson. He went above and beyond to help someone enjoy the game he loves. That's just the way he is.

I've met a lot of people in this game over the past forty-five years, and I can say that Stan is one of the two or three best men I have come to know over that time. I'm lucky to call him my teacher, and I'm proud to call him my friend.

I know he can help you play better and enjoy this game. Isn't that what it's all about?

TOM CISAR
INDIAN HEAD PARK, IL
NOVEMBER 1, 2010

# INTRODUCTION

· · · · · · · · · · · · · · · · · · · · · · · · · · · · · · · · · · · · · · · · · · · · · · · · · ·

O ne of the side benefits that comes with teaching golf full-time—and doing it five minutes from my house, at Grayhawk Golf Club in Scottsdale—is that I can build my lesson schedule in a way that gives me time during the day to spend with my kids.

Last year, I took a late afternoon break to go home and hang out in the driveway with my daughter Tatum. She had decided to try out for her school's basketball team, and I was looking forward to doing a different kind of helping than I'm used to day in and day out around the practice green. Seeing Tatum go to her first practice with some idea of what she was supposed to do was my main goal, but I won't lie—basketball is my first love, and it was only after facing my too-short and too-slow reality as a teenager that I focused on golf as my career.

Tatum and I grabbed the ball and went out to the driveway to work on the basics of shooting a basketball. She's a very focused and coordinated kid, and she picked up the individual mechanical pieces of shooting pretty quickly. She understood how to hold the ball, and how the wrists and arms work. She understood how your legs provide the power to the shot. If you saw a picture of her in the ready position, right before taking the shot, you'd say that she looked like a basketball player.

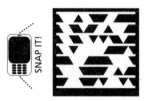

But when it came time to sequence the motion—to fire her legs and release her right arm and put spin on the ball with her right wrist—she had trouble getting things in the right order. Sometimes she'd shoot it over the backboard, and other times the ball would come up three feet short of the rim. And her individual mechanics were great in both cases.

Helping her sort out the sequencing issue got me thinking about my golf teaching, and about the lessons I had gotten—or watched—from other instructors over the years. When a 20-handicapper with some serious short-game problems comes to me looking for help, it's almost automatic to want to sort out his basic setup and stroke mechanics first. And there's solid reasoning behind that. When you have good basic mechanics, it's much, much easier to make a good, repeatable motion.

But mechanics—the "form" of the golf swing—are only one piece of the puzzle. And for many players, they might not even be the most important piece. Tatum had the form of shooting a basketball down. But I think that if she understood how the motion unfolded first and started to get a feel for how to make the ball go as far she wanted it to, with some aim, the mechanics would have been easy to adjust later.

For many people, the golf swing should be no different.

Again, I'm not discounting the importance of mechanics. If you read my first three books and follow the mechanical basics presented there, your short game will improve. But there is a significant piece of the short game—and the full swing—that comes down to sequence of motion. And that's what we're going to talk about in this book.

In *The Art of the Swing*, my goal is to help you understand the relationship between the clubhead and your body, and how all of those parts work with each other. In putts and small short-game shots, the clubhead doesn't move very far and doesn't move very fast, comparatively speaking. But the *way* it moves in relation to your body is the same as it would in a full swing. And if you can understand that relationship in small shots, you can apply it to what you do with your full swing. It doesn't matter if you're hitting a shot ten feet onto the putting green or 230 yards off the tee. The clubhead moves the longest distance compared with your hands and your body, and it needs to move the fastest for your shot to be consistently successful. How you set the clubhead in motion and move your body—in other words, when and how much you move the clubhead in relation to moving your arms, transferring your weight, and pivoting and turning your hips and shoulders—is your swing's "sequence." Good players understand how to make the clubhead move fast in a consistent circle. Bad players move the club and body in the wrong order, making the club move more slowly and on a lopsided or inconsistent circle.

In Chapter 1, I'm going to tell you about form and sequence—what they are and how they should work together in your swing. Even if you haven't read any of my other books, I'll cover enough of the basic mechanics of a putt, short-game shot, and even the full swing so that you can adjust these fundamentals if and when necessary. In the second chapter, we'll talk about the main goal of all of this sequencing: to shift the energy in your swing to the end of the club that hits the ball. There, we'll talk about the major mistakes that players make—usually with the best intentions—and the way energy in the clubhead is important for every shot, from a 10-foot putt to a full-on tee shot with the driver.

Once we've covered the energy part of the equation, we'll talk about control of the clubface in Chapter 3. Once you start moving the end of the club that hits the ball, you can make a series of simple, intuitive moves with your hands and wrists to control the height, direction, and spin on any short-game or full-swing shot. Sequencing is more than just the ordering of physical moves. In Chapter 4, we'll talk about the elements of your pre-round, pre-shot, post-shot and post-round routine, and how they can work together to reduce your score—even if you don't change a thing about your actual mechanics. In the fifth chapter, I'll talk about the concept of swing thoughts or "feels"—how to find them, how to identify the ones that work for you, and how to track them over time and determine when and if you should bring other ones into play.

In Chapter 6, I'll show you how to grow your swing from a putt to a full swing by incorporating many of the same mechanical and sequence elements. How? By hitting five very different shots with the same club. In Chapter 7, we'll move on to the full swing, and I'll explain how improving your short-game sequencing can help smooth out your full swing—as it has for many of my amateur and professional students. In the eighth chapter, we'll talk about reading what the ball tells you, and how to diagnose and make changes to your game—and equipment—based on that information. And in Chapter 9, we'll go over your 30-day plan to reinvent your total game using twenty-minute practice routines that you can perform by themselves or before a round of golf to seamlessly transform yourself into a better player.

One of the challenges in producing a golf book or an instruction article for *Golf Digest* is to actually show a sequence of motion rather than a series of technically accurate "form" positions. Still photographs do a really good job of showing perfect setup positions and the technical checkpoints that happen during a chip shot or an iron shot from the fairway, but it's a challenge to show how to get from one checkpoint to the other. I work with the best in the business—Matt Rudy and J.D. Cuban are staff guys at *Golf Digest,* and they've done hundreds and hundreds of instruction articles there, as well as all four of my books—and the words and pictures you're holding here are going to help your game.

But if you have access to a smartphone with a built-in camera, like an Apple iPhone or a BlackBerry, you have a whole new way to get golf instruction. Using Microsoft's Tag technology, we've connected more than thirty of the photographs in this book with instruction videos. Once you've downloaded the free Tag app for your phone (at either iTunes or http://gettag .mobi on your phone's web browser) you simply activate the app and use your phone's camera to snap a picture of the small square bar code next to each photograph. The instruction video will automatically launch on your phone.

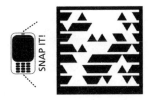

*The Art of the Swing* is the first golf instruction book to combine traditional text and words with customized video instruction. We shot the photographs and videos you see here over a three-day period at the Titleist Performance Institute in Oceanside,

California. The book is designed to make sense—and help your game—as a stand-alone product, but the videos are fully integrated into the printed instruction. In other words, if you're away from your smartphone—or, if you don't have one—you can sit with the book and use it to help your game just the way you have with the previous three books. But if you have your phone handy, you can read the words and look at the photographs, and then get a more complete demonstration and understanding of the concepts with the videos.

Adding a video component to my teaching has been one of the most common requests in the hundreds of e-mails and text messages I've received from readers in response to my first three books, *The Art of Putting, The Art of the Short Game,* and *The Art of Scoring.* I'm really happy to be able to provide video as a part of *The Art of the Swing,* and I'm looking forward to our time together.

Let's get started.

# THE ART OF
# THE SWING

# CHAPTER 1

# FORM VS. SEQUENCE

· · · · · · · · · · · · · · · · · · · · · · · · · · · · · · · · · · · · · · · · · ·

So what are form and sequence, and how do they work together in your golf swing? Understanding the difference between the two—and how they're related—will make the process of improving your game much, much simpler.

To make the motion of swinging a club—whether it's for a putt, a little chip shot, a 7-iron shot from the fairway, or a tee shot with a driver—you start by putting your hands on the club a certain way and setting up and aligning your body in a certain way. Whether you're making a conscious decision about it or not, you're distributing your weight in a certain way, flexing your knees and elbows to a certain degree, and bending over to the ball a certain amount.

And as you make that motion, your body and the club move through certain checkpoints at given moments during the motion. If we took video of your swing, we could freeze the image at those checkpoints and make a pretty accurate analysis of what you were doing right and wrong. "Form" is how your body and club positions compare with those of an ideal swing.

Now, what makes up perfect form, or an ideal swing? There are some fundamentals that are pretty much universal—and I'm going to talk about a few of them later in this chapter, in case you haven't read about them in my first three books. But people aren't stamped out of the same cookie cutter, and neither are golf swings. Your body type and size, fitness level, flexibility level, and playing experience all play a role in determining what perfect "form" is for you.

An overwhelming amount of printed golf instruction has been devoted to form—getting you to set up in the right position, and prompting you to match certain perfect positions during the swing. I've devoted chapters to form in my previous three books and in my *Golf Digest* articles. This strategy isn't wrong. It's just not the whole story. Having perfect form in terms of how you set your body and the club at address is helpful, and understanding where the club should be at the top of your backswing and at impact is important. But good form basics only make it easier to execute the main mission—to move the club and body in the right sequence for the shot at hand.

Form is what makes it easier for you to hit the kind of shot you intend to hit consistently. Sequence is what gives you the ability to actually make the ball move. In a golf swing, the clubhead, the hands, and the body all move in their own circular path—a concept I'm going to tell you a lot more about in the next chapter. A player with good sequencing moves the clubhead, hands, and body around in these circles at the right time, in the right amounts, and in the right proportion, depending on the shot at hand. Good sequencing is the reason why you can watch a tour player make a seemingly effortless swing and hit the ball 300 yards—the speed of his or her clubhead is magnified by the physics of an efficient chain reaction of energy being released.

Some of the "secrets" of swing sequencing will undoubtedly surprise you. You can have good-looking form and bad sequencing and be a terrible golfer your entire life. But even if you have strange-looking form, you can be a good player if you understand the order in which the clubhead, hands, and body should move for a given shot. In other words, if you generate energy on the end of the club that hits the ball with a somewhat square clubface, you can play this game—even if your form limits the variety of shots you can hit. I've seen players who hit a low hook on every full shot and play almost every short-game shot along the ground. But they understand sequencing, and they play to the kind of shots they know they're going to hit, and they shoot around par. You're probably wondering if learning good sequencing is difficult, or if it's a skill available to only super-talented players. Not only is it relatively simple—and accessible for any player—it can be found through a window of small shots that you can hit at any practice green. That's right. The shots of the short game—a putt, a chip shot, a lofted pitch, and a bunker shot—contain smaller examples of good swing sequencing through impact. You can train yourself in good sequencing on smaller, slower swings and incorporate that knowledge into your full swing—and hit the ball longer, straighter, and more consistently.

In my other books, we talked a lot about form, and about picking the right kinds of shots to hit for certain circumstances. In this book, I'm going to touch on a few important form basics as a starting point, but the bulk of the information I'm going to share—both in print and in the videos that go with the pictures—is how to move your body and club in the right sequence. Even if you've read my other three books, it'll probably be helpful for you to go through the rest of this chapter and brush up on a few of the form basics for putting and the short game—and to hear what I've learned about the full swing over the past few years through my work with some fantastic teachers.

Like I said, the information over the next few pages is a form checkpoint—a place to start if you're looking for guidance on a

I can describe the best position for the club to be in through impact on a low chip shot—left wrist bowed, clubhead releasing but hands still ahead, and weight favoring the front foot—but getting in the right position moment by moment isn't the same as understanding the dynamic relationship between your body and the club throughout the swing.

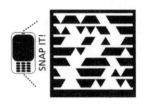

SNAP IT!

better way to put your hands on the club or stand to the ball. Good form is certainly important and helpful in making your game more consistent, but good sequencing is what separates the good players from the not-so-good ones.

## GRIP FORM

The way you hold onto the club is the fundamental form element for any shot, from a putt to a full swing—and it's the fundamental that can have the most impact on your ability to sequence the club properly for the shot you're trying to hit. Let me give you the basic hows and whys of the putting and full-swing grips, and the differences between the two.

Extend your hand out in front of you in line with your arm and with your palm flat. Now experiment with hinging your wrist. You'll quickly see that the wrist joint can move in two different ways. You can hinge the wrist up and down, like a miniature handshake move. You can hinge it back and forth like you're slapping something. You can also twist your forearms as if you're turning a screwdriver. Ideally, you would take advantage of all of these different flavors of movement to hit a variety of different shots. The goal in terms of your grip is to give yourself the most neutral, easy platform to promote the kind of wrist and forearm action you want for the shot at hand.

Let's start with putting. On a putt, you have to be very sensitive to how the face is aimed and to the "feel" of the clubhead. I teach that it's okay to use a little wrist action in your stroke, but that the wrists only move in a slightly side-to-side action. You wouldn't ever need them to work up and down to produce the kind of power needed for a full swing. A good putting grip does exactly that—it puts your hands on the club in a neutral position and retains the touch and feel in your fingers so that the use of a little wrist action will allow you to swing the club on a path that doesn't require you to manipulate the face to hit solid and square putts.

Stand in a comfortable position and let your hands hang down naturally at your sides. The way your left hand hangs— loosely and comfortably next to your leg—is the basis for how it should go on your putter grip. Your right hand should connect to the left so that if you open it up flat it would face the intended start line of the putt. If your hands are in this neutral position—facing each other and square to the target line, not rotated closed or open to the target, or turned independent of each other—it's much easier to keep them (and the clubface) that way. If one or both of your hands is turned into a non-neutral position on the grip, you will not be able to freely swing the putterhead without otherwise manipulating the club during the stroke to recalibrate whatever aim you set up at address.

To build a neutral grip, start by holding the putter up in front of you with your right hand positioned on the shaft just under the grip and the face vertical to the ground. Now squeeze your left thumb down toward the palm of your hand. Notice how easy it is to identify the lifeline in your left hand at this point. I want you to place your thumb down along the top of your putter grip so that it presses firmly against the lifeline. I would rather you make a mistake with your left hand turned a little more to the right than the left. Now it's time for your right hand to find its place. Your goal is to have your right palm face the start line of the putt and at the same time have your hand, wrist, and right forearm in line with the shaft plane.

One big difference in how your hands go together with this grip and your swing grip is the placement of the lifeline on your right hand. With a swing grip it will connect with your thumb. In a neutral grip, your lifeline needs to connect with the last knuckle of your middle finger as shown in the pictures. This placement will give you the best chance of getting the shaft and your forearms on the same plane and the top of your forearms level and aiming parallel with your start line. The last step is to have your left index finger extend and wrap comfortably around the outside of the little finger on your right hand. I've been using this exact same reverse-overlap putting grip ever since my first teacher, Mr. Lanning, taught it to me thirty years ago.

The feel you're looking for is that of your fingertips being the main contact point on the grip. Your fingertips have the most nerve endings in your entire body, and they're the foundation of touch and feel. With this grip, you're in position to be far more sensitive to what's happening with the club. This fingertip-centered grip also encourages you to hold onto the

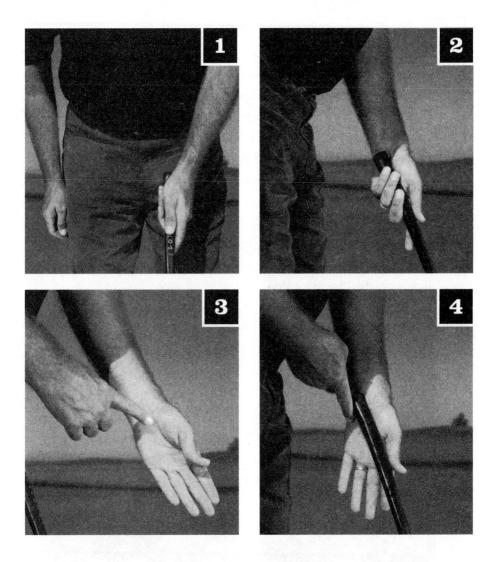

In a putting grip, you want your hands to be parallel to each other and square to the target line. To start, build your left-hand grip with your thumb on top of the putter (1). Many putting grips are built with a flat top for exactly this purpose. When the putter is in your left hand, the grip should point along your forearm (2). To find this sweet spot in your palm, slightly flex the base of your thumb to puff up the muscle (3). Then, with your hand pointed down, the grip runs underneath this thumb pad (4).

putter much more loosely, which relaxes your arms and shoulders—another feel-promoting benefit.

As I mentioned before, once you've built this neutral grip, the tops of your forearms should be in line, parallel with your target. Have a friend take another club and hold it lightly on your forearms, three or four inches above where you'd wear your watch. The club should point parallel to the target line. If your grip falls out of neutral, one forearm or the other will get higher or lower, and the club across your forearms will point left or right of your target. I believe that putting from this position will affect the path of your backswing in a way that will force you to loop the putter or otherwise manipulate the face to get the ball back on line.

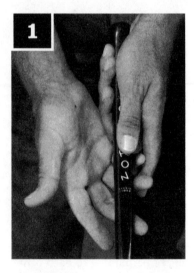 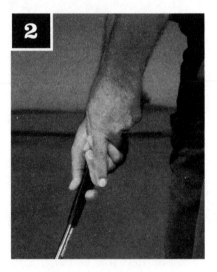

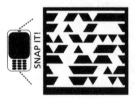

Once you've set your left-hand putting grip, wrap your right hand around the handle (1). Notice the small dot I've made on my right palm, at the base of my lifeline. This dot should connect with the last knuckle of the middle finger on your left hand. The thumb on the right hand will angle over and connect on top of the putter grip alongside the left thumb. When the grip is formed, the index finger of your left hand will run over the fingers on the right (2).

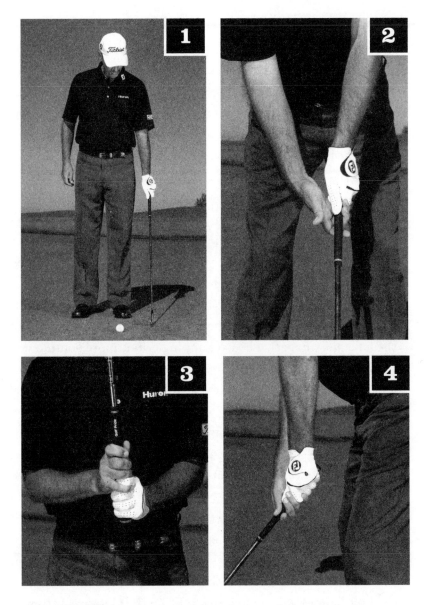

When you set your grip for a full swing, you have to take into account that your hands hang at your sides at a slight angle, not straight down (1). Sole the club flat on the ground and set your grip with your left hand first. Once your left hand is on the club, incorporate your right hand onto the grip (2). In an interlocking grip, the pinky finger of the right hand lies between the big knuckles on the left hand (3). While the club points up the forearm in a putting grip, it points under the arms on a full swing (4) because the handle is resting more in the fingers.

How does this grip compare with the one you use for the rest of your shots? It's completely different, and for good reason. On short-game shots and full swings, the wrists are an important speed-generating component. The grip you use needs to reinforce that goal. Instead of running along the lifeline and lining up with the forearms, the handle of the club needs to sit along the base of the fingers. That allows you to hinge your wrists up and down—like you would if you were casting a fishing line.

Just like the putting grip, your short-game and full-swing grips should be neutral, with your palms opposing each other the way they would with your arms hanging at your sides. You can link your hands together with either an overlapping grip (the pinky finger of the right hand rests on top of the left hand, between the knuckles of the index and middle fingers) or the interlocking grip (the pinky finger on the right hand links with the left index finger). The overlapping grip is more common on the PGA Tour, but Tiger Woods and Jack Nicklaus have won a lot of tournaments interlocking. I think it's a matter of personal preference.

One of the best ways to find your proper grip is to try this exercise: Start with your left arm hanging next to your side. Notice how your hand lays naturally in a position that is rotated slightly toward your left leg. Now lay the grip in the fingers of your left hand and make sure the leading edge of the clubface is parallel to your feet. With the grip running along the first joint of your fingers (where they meet your palm), squeeze your hand down onto the grip with your thumb pressed up against the first joint of your index finger. Bring the club up in front of you to set your right-hand grip. Place the grip along the first joints of the fingers on your right hand, and put the right palm down so that the lifeline runs down your left thumb. This gives you the freedom to accelerate the clubhead and the ability to square the face naturally through impact.

The relative strength or weakness of your grip determines how easy or hard it is to rotate your forearms and release the club through impact. With a weak grip, the forearms need to rotate a lot through impact to square the face, while the opposite is true with a strong grip. You can certainly play successful golf with either one, but I believe that a neutral grip gives you the best combination of power and control. I use a neutral grip and modify my forearm rotation and wrist action to create different shots. By rotating my forearms more and bowing my left wrist, I take loft off the face and hit low shots. By restricting rotation and releasing the clubhead early, I can produce a higher shot (more on that in Chapter 3).

To check the strength of your grip, hold the club straight out in front of you and hinge it up and down using only your wrists. If your grip is neutral, the leading edge of the clubface will move straight up and down, perpendicular to the ground. If you hinge the club up and down and the toe tilts left of the heel, you have a strong grip. If the toe tilts to the right, you have a weak grip.

## SETUP FORM

"Neutral" and "natural" are words I like to use to describe a good setup position for any shot. There are some differences from a putt to a chip shot to a full swing—width of stance, weight distribution—but I want to start with the parameters that extend to virtually any shot, with the possible exceptions of a shot from a deep bunker or a super-high flop shot. When you stand naturally and have a conversation with somebody, you most likely set your feet fairly close together. That natural width—about four or five inches at the heels—is the stance width I like for putting. I keep this same width for most of my short-game shots around the green. On full-swing shots, my feet get wider, to hip-width. My heels are about 10 inches apart for my iron shots and about 14 inches apart for a driver.

Mike Adams showed me a great way to find the most athletic stance width. He first asked me to make a standing long jump. As soon as I set my feet to make the jump he stopped me to show how I had naturally found my best stance width. If you try to jump with your feet too close together or spread very wide, you simply won't be as explosive. Most players try this drill and discover that their stance is set too wide.

When the stance gets too wide (and the ball position stays near the center, as it does on a putt, chip, or middle-iron shot), the tendency is for the shoulders to rock up and down instead of turn—a recipe for inconsistent contact. On any shot, you need to have an athletic flex in your legs—as though you were getting ready to shoot a basketball or field a one-hopper in baseball—and to tilt forward from your hip sockets. Many players struggle because they slump their shoulders, curve their spine, and bend from the waist instead of tilting from the hips. All that does is restrict the body's ability to turn, and the swing becomes a weaker, arm-dominated move. My good friend, teacher, and tour pro, Tom Kalinowski, tells me he thinks the reason my putting is so good is that my setup is solid. His point is that any technique you use from a balanced setup—narrow, square, even, weight distributed evenly, elbows soft and not extended and rigid—is going to work better, not just the technique that I teach.

In a good putting setup position, lines drawn in front of my toes, knees, hips and shoulders would all point parallel to the target line (1). My arms are hanging softly from my shoulders. They aren't rigid or tight. Most importantly, I'm bending from the hips, not slumping my spine forward toward the ball (2). From the front view (3), you can see that my feet are set narrowly, only four inches apart, and the shaft is fairly vertical. The club is in the middle of my stance, and the ball is just ahead of center. I trigger my swing by starting with a slight forward press of my hands toward the target.

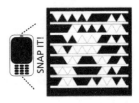

SNAP IT!

In a pitching setup, my stance is nearly the same width as it would be on a putt (1), and the ball occupies the same position—just ahead of center.

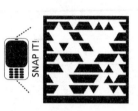

SNAP IT!

The next two pieces of the setup are related—ball position and shaft angle. On a putt, I like to have the face of my putter in the middle of my stance and the ball just ahead of the putterface. The shaft is at 90-degree angle to the ground at setup and then presses slightly forward to jump-start my stroke. This position is pretty much the same as the one I use for a standard chip or pitch shot, or for a short- to middle-iron shot, with my stance getting slightly wider as the shot gets longer. Many players struggle with shots around the green because they set up with the ball back in the stance (usually because they've heard you have to hit down on the ball). A common putting setup issue is having the putter leaning backward, away from the target. I believe this problem often arises when the player is using a putter with too little loft and instinctively moves the shaft back to be able to see more of the face. When you move the shaft backward that way at the setup, it basically guarantees

When you move to a full wedge shot, the setup position grows into that of a regular full swing. My feet get a little wider—to hip width—and I have a little more knee flex to account for that (1). On a wedge shot, I set up square (2), which keeps the swing on plane and makes square clubface contact more likely.

that you'll move the wrong end of the club—the grip end—to start the swing. Pushing the shaft slightly forward at address is not a problem, but just know that doing it reduces the effective loft of any club you use, whether it's a putter or a wedge. Also, it's important to know that it's difficult to start with 90-degree shaft lean if the ball position is too far forward at setup.

The problem with ball position is that the phrase itself implies that the ball moves back and forth depending on the shot. I suppose that's technically true, but I look at it a different way. I don't move the ball as much as I keep the ball in the same place relative

With a 6-iron (1), my stance gets still wider—just outside hip width—and you can see I have slightly more shoulder tilt away from the target. My ball position has moved slightly more forward, and my hands are set just forward of my zipper. Notice how my posture is consistent with how I've set up for a short pitch shot in the previous set of pictures (2). The only changes to my spine angle come on a putt, a lofted shot, or with a driver.

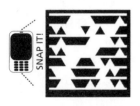

My stance gets wider on a driver, but not dramatically so. If you set your feet any wider than just outside your shoulders, as I have here (1), you start to hinder your ability to make a full hip turn. Draw a line straight down from my chin and that's where my swing will bottom out—just behind the ball. My spine angle is slightly more upright with the driver (2) than with a middle iron.

to my head and adjust the width of my feet. The only exception is with the driver, where the ball actually does get played off the inside heel of my front foot. Otherwise, on a putt, I'm using a relatively narrow stance, while I use a wider stance—moving my back foot away from the target, but keeping the ball in the same place relative to my belt buckle and my head—for a full-iron shot.

Here you can see the dramatic setup changes that go into hitting a super-high shot—or a bunker shot, which is hit the same way. I take a wide stance, wider than with my driver (1), and move my hands back so that the shaft is angled slightly backward. This exposes the bounce on the bottom of the club, and increases the effective loft. Notice how level my shoulders are. Players who struggle tend to let the right shoulder drop at address and scoop at the ball. By lowering my hands and moving farther away from the ball (2), I have created more loft on the clubface. I have not opened my stance. I'm aimed right at the target, and I don't have to compensate for side spin like players who play this shot from an open stance with an open clubface do.

Where you set your chin determines the bottom of your swing arc (1). On short game shots, the bottom of your swing should be in front of the ball, so you can contact the ball with a descending blow. The natural loft of the club will get the ball in the air without any help. If you set up with your head and weight back (2), or move your weight back there during the swing, you will bottom out behind the ball and either skull it or hit it fat.

Setup and ball position only change dramatically for three shots—a driver or fairway wood off a tee, a bunker shot, or a lofted pitch. We've already talked about the ball-position change you need for a driver. Setup-wise, I use a wide stance—with my feet slightly wider than my shoulders, to support a bigger, more aggressive shoulder turn—and I flare my feet out slightly. Doing that makes it easier for me to turn my hips going back and through. Because of the more forward ball position, I also have more shoulder tilt than with any other shot. The longer club pushes me farther from the ball at address, and I have to make a correspondingly flatter swing.

When you set up this way with your driver, you're using your weight distribution across your feet to establish the bottom of your swing arc. With a driver, the swing bottoms out before the ball and you're hitting it slightly on the upswing. For that shot, your weight is even across both feet, or possibly a little more on the back foot at address. Your ball position is forward, just inside the left heel. On an iron shot, your weight is centered over your feet, and the bottom of the swing happens just in front of the ball. On short-game shots, you shift your weight more to your forward foot—65 or 70 percent—which moves the bottom of the swing in front of the ball, so that you're hitting the ball first and then the ground. Many, many short-game problems happen when you either start with your weight back or you shift it that way when you try to scoop the ball into the air.

The only really dramatic setup changes happen when you need to hit a shot with more loft. I use the exact same setup and technique for a bunker shot as I do for an extra-high pitch or a trouble shot from a sketchy lie. The goal is to get the clubhead moving faster and to increase the effective loft of the club through impact. To do that, spread your feet out wide—wider than you would to hit a driver, and bow your knees, almost as though you were sitting in a chair. Instead of tilting your shoulders away from the target, like you would with a driver, tilt them toward the target. Keep your ball position a little ahead of the middle of your stance, but move farther away from the ball than standard, so you have to bend over more from the waist toward the ball. This also increases the effective loft of the club. What does the correct spine tilt for this shot feel like? Try this drill. Set your feet shoulder-width apart and bend your knees. Hold your club in your right hand. Now slide your left hand down the side of your leg until you touch your left knee. Your shoulders will then have the proper tilt.

Alignment is another setup fundamental in which making a mistake can wreak havoc on your game. A small alignment mistake can throw off a 15-foot putt by six inches—more than enough to miss—and the mistake just compounds as the club gets longer. And alignment is more than just where your feet are aimed. How you have your feet aligned versus your hips and shoulders also determines where your shot ends up.

On a putt, I try to set up with everything square. If you drew a line in front of the tips of my shoes, it would run parallel to the target line, as would a line across my hips and shoulders. Setting up slightly closed—with the line in front of your toes pointing to the right of the target line—is okay, but it means that you're going to have to account for that change when you aim and make your stroke. I don't recommend using an open stance. Some players like it because it gives them the feeling of being able to see the line better, but I don't like the way it promotes wiping across the ball with an open putterface.

By far the biggest alignment issues start to crop up in the short game. Many, many players have been taught that you need to set up open to the target at address, with the feet and shoulders aimed to the left of the target and the ball moved back in the stance. The ball position by itself makes that shot way harder than it needs to be—you're encouraging the leading edge of the club to dig into the ground instead of using the bounce on the bottom of the club the way it was designed— and the open shoulders and feet mean you have to do something with the swing to compensate for the fact that you're not aimed at the target. It also encourages you to take the club back outside the target line, away from your body. The only way to hit a good shot from there is to scoop with your hands or block it toward the target.

The same problem crops up in bunker play. Players are taught to open their stance and play the ball way forward, with an open clubface. Although I have seen this technique work nicely for some players, I think it adds more variables to the equation than is necessary. Many years ago, PGA Tour player Tom Pernice gave me my first bunker lesson. He showed me a method that allows for a fairly square stance and clubface. By widening your stance and moving away from the ball a bit, you achieve all the same goals, but without changing where your body and the club are aimed. It's fun to hit your bunker shot and see the ball check up and the release straight to the hole.

On full swings, both with the irons and the driver, many players change their alignment in an effort to compensate for their regular ball-flight tendency. I've played a lot of pro-ams and corporate golf rounds. I see a lot of slicers, and almost without exception the person with a big left-to-right curve on their shot is aiming way to the left. This might make sense if you're trying to play the curve of your shot and still find the fairway, but it doesn't fix the problem. The more left you aim, the more your instincts kick in to swing across the ball to make it come back to the right. It's a vicious cycle. The simple act of making a few swings aimed straight or even to the right will cause you to change your swing path to a more neutral shot with less curve. That's a simplification, but it works.

I like a neutral alignment on full shots, just as I do on short-game and putting shots. I also want you to learn what a square clubface looks like at setup. I see a lot of players who fight a slice setup with the clubface very closed. This promotes an up and out backswing and then an opening move of the clubface coming through impact. This just leads to more slicing. Mike Adams showed me how to set up a practice station on the driving range to help learn what square looks like. Pick a target and lay a club on the ground about three to four feet in front of the ball you're going to hit, aimed straight at the target (you could even stick one of those thin snow guide poles from the hardware store in the ground eight steps in front of the ball to get a really good sense of your target). Now place a club on the ground near where your feet will be at setup and make it parallel to the one out in front of the ball. These tools will help your eyes get used to squarely aligning your body. Once you know that your setup is good, it's just a matter of learning how to make the correct swing to produce a good shot. If you're having trouble seeing progress on your own, it might be time to go see a good teacher in your area for another set of eyes.

## SWING FORM

We're going to cover all of the actual mechanics of how to hit the important short- and long-game shots in chapters 6 and 7, but I want to give you a brief overview here so you can understand the difference between the "form" positions during the swing and the fluid, dynamic sequencing of your body in a swing.

A putt is obviously the smallest stroke you can make, but it still has a sequence of motion to it that does not necessarily come through in photographs. As I said, I start my stroke with a slight forward press, then hinge my right wrist slightly and let my right elbow slide against my side. This causes the putter to move along a slight arc. Then the putter drops from the top of the backswing with almost no conscious muscle effort and my left elbow then softens and slides along my left side. The follow-through is short and low to the grass—all the energy has been spent right at the ball. You can put the putter in the right position at the top of the mini-backswing, at impact, or at the finish, but that's different than moving it there in flowing sequence.

Now let's use the example of a full-wedge shot—one where you would make a full backswing but in a slower, smaller way than a driver swing. For the clubhead to move on the correct path in the backswing, your arms move the club back as your upper body turns and your weight stays fairly centered, although

This is a great position to copy—slightly hinged right wrist, clubhead at the top of the backswing with the grip end not moving much at all—but it doesn't tell the story of how the clubhead got to where it is, or what it will do next.

it does shift slightly to the back foot in the backswing. At the top of the backswing, good form dictates about a 65-degree shoulder turn and about a 30-degree hip turn. The wrists are hinged—so that the club is in an "L" shape relative to the left arm—and the back of the left wrist is flat. The spine is also at the same angle at the top of the backswing as it was at address.

For a full-wedge shot, you set up square to the target (1) and make a full-degree shoulder turn at the top of the backswing (2). The arms stay soft, not rigid, and the club does not reach parallel. I have not restricted my hip turn—I let them turn in response to my shoulders turning back. On the through-swing (3), my hips and shoulders have fully turned and released, and I'm balanced on my front foot. I don't come up out of my posture until the ball is long gone.

Down through impact, the handle of the club should lean forward slightly, and your weight should pivot from your back foot to your front foot. The hips and shoulders don't stop turning, and they continue around until virtually all of your weight is on the front foot and the energy in the swing is gone. If you've made a smooth, balanced transfer, you should be able to end your swing and easily hold your finish position with the club over your left shoulder. In a swing that has fully unwound, the belt buckle is pointing at the target, while the shoulders have actually turned a little past the target.

By describing these positions, I've given you a map of a good golf swing. But just like making a cross-country car trip, the trick is actually getting from point A to point B. Many, many players have good setup fundamentals and get to a balanced finish position, but they don't move their arms, body, and club in the right sequence, and they don't get the consistent results they want. Our goal here is to mix good static fundamentals and form with a better idea for sequencing. Match the two of those and you're on your way.

# CHAPTER 2

# MOVING ENERGY TO THE CLUBHEAD

W hen I demonstrate a basic bunker shot at a clinic, the overwhelming response I get from the average amateur player is that it "looks easy." I've heard the same comment a hundred times while walking practice rounds with Sergio Garcia, or any number of other tour players, after they've hit a towering 5-iron to the green or a driver off the tee.

Now, I'm not trying to minimize what goes into being able to hit shots like that. It definitely takes great technique and a lot of practice and experience. But when you understand how the club should work—and how and where to produce the energy necessary to hit a shot—it *is* much easier. Certainly much easier than many players make it for themselves. My fundamental goal in this book is to help you develop your sense for how and when to build and release energy in the clubhead through impact. It happens in two basic steps—moving the energy in your swing to the clubhead (not the grip), and controlling the clubface through impact. We're going to cover those two steps in the next two chapters.

I realize I've been throwing around the term "energy" a lot here. What does "energy" mean when it comes to a golf swing? Basically, energy is speed. Moving the clubhead makes the ball go farther (or higher). It also has a hidden benefit that even many good players don't understand. To move the clubhead faster, one end of the club—the grip—has to be moving less and slower than the other end. By making the clubhead end move faster, you're allowing the club to move the way it was designed. The head flies through the air in a very precise arc determined by centrifugal force and physics. If you aim that arc correctly at the start, you can essentially get out of the way and let physics hit the shot for you.

I realize that this idea may sound daunting at first. What in the world does anybody know about physics? And learning to move energy to the clubhead in the swing is definitely about giving up the idea that most people have about *controlling* the club. Most players instinctively try to move the handle end of the club to make the clubhead end do what they think it's supposed to do during the swing. That's understandable, but it isn't very efficient. To make the clubhead end move fast, you have to let go of the idea of controlling the grip end and start to think more about leverage and multiplication of effort and speed.

I'm going to show you how to do that here.

Let's start with the concept of three circles. For all the information you've heard about the golf swing—including what you heard from me in the last chapter—for simplification's sake let's say the basic motion comes down to three circles. Your body moves in the first, smallest circle, in the form of your hip and shoulder turn. The hands and grip move in the second circle—which is a little bigger than the first one because it's happening at the end of your arms. The biggest circle is the one being traced by the clubhead, which is obviously extended from your hands and the grip by the length of the shaft.

In order for the clubhead to get to the ball when you make a swing, I think we can all agree that the clubhead has to travel the longest distance. To hit effective golf shots—whether they're on the putting green, from the tee, in the fairway, or from a bunker—you have to sequence the points on the three circles so that they arrive at the ball at the right time, and in the right order.

When you watch Ernie Els effortlessly hit a 300-yard tee shot, it doesn't look like he's expending very much energy. But there's no doubt that there's a lot of speed on his clubhead. The reason his swing is so efficient—and produces so much power—is because he's moving the three circles in perfect sequence.

Players struggle when they move the points in the circle in the wrong sequence—moving the clubhead too fast from the top of the downswing, before the body turns, for example, or turning the body aggressively on the downswing while the club trails too far behind—or when they change the location of the circles themselves. We're going to address both of those problems here.

Before we do that, I want to help you get a sense of exactly what the goal is here—to really feel what it means to speed up the clubhead. Because, like I said, the whole purpose of any golf swing is to deliver the clubhead to the ball in a predictable way, with enough speed to make the ball go the distance you want. Most players have spent so many years either consciously or unconsciously swinging their body and the grip end of the club hard or aggressively while never experiencing what clubhead speed really is. To feel it, try this drill. Take a heavy club like a pitching wedge or a sand wedge and hold it in your standard grip. Lay the club on your right shoulder and keep your hands near your belly button. Make some swings that are simply a shoulder turn and an unhinging of your wrists down and then up again, returning the club to your left shoulder. As you practice this move, try to get the club moving faster and faster, but without moving your hands away from your middle.

The snap of your wrists in this isolated drill is exactly what teachers and players mean when they talk about "releasing" the clubhead on a full shot. It's not just rolling the wrists over or turning them like a screwdriver. It's this downward snap that generates speed on the clubhead end. This can't happen if you

**On a full swing, the upper body (represented by my right hand in the middle of my chest (1) moves the shortest distance, making a small circle (2).**

Compare the distance the hands and grip make in the same size swing from the address position (1) with waist high (2) and to the top of the backswing on a short iron shot. The buttons on my shirt have moved about eight inches, while my hands have traveled about four feet.

The clubhead moves the largest distance around a big circle—from the address position (1) to waist high (2), it has moved probably eight feet, and then another six feet to the top of the backswing (3). The location of these three circles, along with where the points on the circles intersect, determines the quality of your swing.

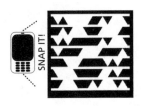

A sequencing mistake is to move the hands in much too large of a circle in the takeaway compared with the body (1), which leads to an awkward compensation at the top of the backswing (2). If the body turns too fast and too early in the downswing (3), it forces you to shift the hands forward through impact, which slows down the clubhead (4).

When you drag the grip backward on the backswing (1), the most common compensation is to shift the weight back as well in a misguided effort to scoop the ball into the air with the hands (2). But shifting your weight this way moves the bottom of the circle the clubhead makes to a spot way behind the ball. You'll skull it or hit it fat from there.

continue to pull the grip end of the club to the target without ever allowing the clubhead to catch up at impact.

Another way to think about this wrist snap is to imagine how you would crack a whip or cast a fishing line. If you hold the whip and try to move the handle out and away from your body, you can't make the business end of the whip snap. It's only when the handle stops that the opposite end can move fast. The same is true for a fishing rod. You sling the lure out into the stream by loading the flexible rod and stopping the handle with a change of direction. The more the handle end moves in the same direction that you want the lure to go, the shorter the lure actually travels.

Once you've felt the snap of the clubhead, the next step is to establish in which direction that snap happens on a given shot. We're going to go into more detail for particular shots in the next few chapters, but I'll give you a brief overview of some of the different ways the wrists can move here, so you can get the basic principle.

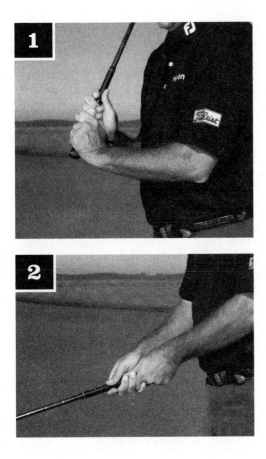

To get a feel for how the wrists should hinge and unhinge on a full shot, hold your hands in front of your chest and put the club up by your right shoulder (1). Then snap your wrists straight down so the club is in line with your forearms. Add a tilt and a turn to this movement and you will have made a full release (2).

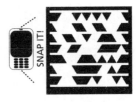

The up and down hinging of the wrists you just practiced in the drill above is how they work for a full shot—everything from a 90-yard wedge to a driver off the tee. How aggressively you unhinge them is one more method in your repertoire of distance control. Some shots require a very fast release, and others you want your hand and wrist action to be more quiet. When you hear Tiger Woods talk about hitting a "dead-arm" shot into a green, he's talking about hitting a shot with a not very aggressive unhinging of the wrists through impact. He has the strength to swing both hard and fast, but most of us average golfers go too far, to the point where extra effort actually makes the clubhead slow down.

The wrist can also move back and forth—hinging in the place where the edge of your watch would hit. This hinge comes into play mostly on putts, where the right wrist hinges on the backswing to let the putter swing back on the correct plane. The third way the wrists hinge is "under"— they're unhinging in a similar way to the full shot, but both hands are turned away from the target so the move is more like the one you would use to skip a rock along the surface of the water.

I want to differentiate a wrist "twist" from a wrist "hinge." You can also make your forearms and wrists rotate or twist or roll through impact. In fact, many players believe that twisting the wrists like a screwdriver or letting the forearms roll over equates to releasing the clubhead. If you learn to unhinge your wrists in the correct sequence, the rotation of your forearms will begin to happen much more naturally, and you won't have to keep them so active before impact. I twist my wrists slightly through impact to turn down the face and change the effective loft on the clubhead, but that's a subject for the next chapter. It's not as much related to creating speed as it is to controlling trajectory.

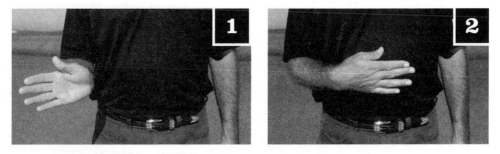

The wrists can hinge back (1) and forth (2) along the joint where your watch would sit on your right arm. This hinge is the one you would use in your putting stroke.

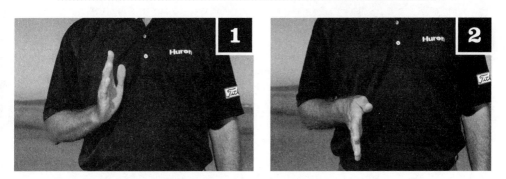

The wrists hinge up (1) and down (2) in a full swing, providing the maximum leverage and "crack" of the whip through impact.

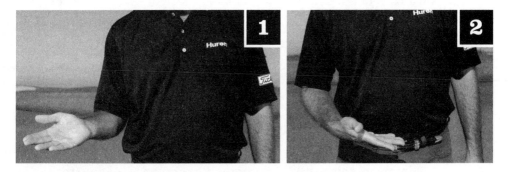

This wrist hinge is similar to the up and down one used on a full swing, but is made with the hands turned away from the target. Moving the club back (1) and forth (2) this way on a bunker shot or a lofted pitch feels like skipping a rock across the water.

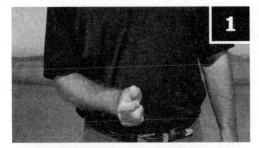

**This shows the loading of the right wrist on the takeaway (2) and the turning down of the right wrist (3) as you would for a low shot.**

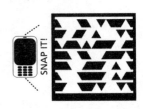

One of the best ways to understand the variety of ways the circles work together—and how the wrists contribute to the circles moving in sequence—is to start with the smallest swing. On a 10-foot putt, the smallest circle—the body—barely moves at all. Using the method I teach, the hands and grip should barely move in relation to the belt buckle, but the right wrist should hinge as the right elbow softens and bends. This freedom of movement in the joints is what allows the clubhead to move a much greater distance. On the downswing, the shoulders and body move the least, while the arms and wrists swing the clubhead so that it moves the longest distance.

Compare this with an extremely common situation that players get themselves into with the putter when a teacher or a friend tells them their stroke is too "wristy." The first thing they do is stiffen the wrists and move the grip end of the putter back with the arms. They get to the top of the backswing, and the only way to generate enough energy to hit the ball is to shove the grip end toward the ball first and then flip the club at the ball with the wrists—the exact "wristiness" they've been trying to avoid.

I would argue that players who move the grip that way are actually "wristy backward." I think the wrists need to play a part in every swing, and using them correctly and in the right sequence actually creates a sounder, more efficient strike on the ball—whether it's on a putt or on a full shot.

The problem of shifting the grip end of the putter is a common one for even tour players, who spend as much time trying to control the stroke as average players do. I've worked with dozens of professionals on this problem, and I start most of them out the same way I'd start you if we had a visit. I drop three or four balls down on the green and ask the player to hold the putter in only the right hand and knock the balls across the green. Very quickly, the player picks up on the fact that shifting the grip just doesn't work when you don't have two hands on the club to support it. The only way to make the ball move is to load the putter with the wrist and let the head swing. That feeling is exactly the one you want on a putt (and a short-game shot), but sized to fit the shot at hand.

When you move on to 20- or 30-yard chips and pitches, you're simply applying the same technique, but you're growing it a little bit by adding a small pivot to account for the longer shot. One of the cornerstone drills I use with players of every level is to set up and hit simple low chip shots using body turn through impact to control distance. With this drill, you make a slight hip and shoulder turn on the backswing and hinge the right wrist and elbow—keeping the hands and grip directly in

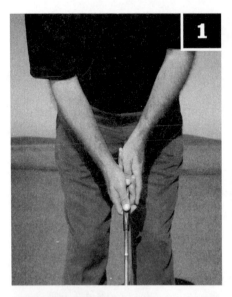

On a short swing like a putt, it's very easy to see what the body and hands should—and shouldn't—do in terms of sequence. From the address position (1) to the top of the backswing (2), my body has barely moved, and my hands have hardly changed position. My right wrist has hinged, but the butt of the club is still pointed in the same place. At the finish (3) the grip has moved slightly forward after my right wrist has released back to the address position.

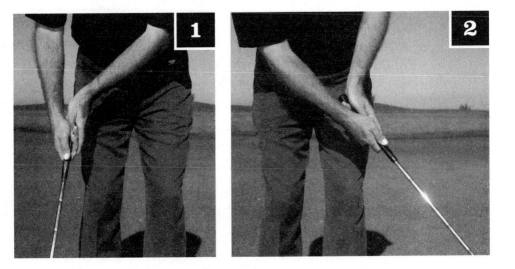

Contrast the previous pictures with this common example. In an effort to combat a "wristy" stroke, many players lock their wrists and shift the entire putter back in the backswing (1). The only way to get the putter onto the ball with any energy is to shift the entire putter back and flip the clubhead so it doesn't hit the ground (2).

A fantastic way to develop a feel for loading and unloading the putter in the right sequence is to hit putts across the green one-handed. It's impossible to shift the grip and generate enough energy to do it successfully.

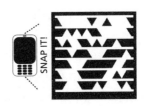

SNAP IT!

front of your belt. The clubhead unloads back to the ball as you release your wrist and right elbow while turning the lower body back through to a low, controlled finish. The faster and larger the shoulder turn and you pivot through, the longer the shot will travel. You can get extremely comfortable and extremely consistent with this shot in a short time. Most players I teach pick it up in thirty minutes, and feel as though they've suddenly developed a little "default" chip shot that they can use even under the most pressure-packed situations.

The changes I make to my bunker-shot setup are designed to affect the angle of attack on the ball at impact. You want to use a lot of wrist action to create speed and to expose the bounce of the club at impact. Start with a wide stance, with your hands set low and a slight tilt of the spine toward the target. It's crucial to maintain the left tilt of the spine throughout the swing, even though it may feel like a reverse pivot to you. But it helps make the downward blow you need on a sand shot easier to create. Although the sequence of turning your body is much different on a sand shot, I still want you to turn back and through. Focus on making a big hip turn in the takeaway, and remember that you should maintain your left tilt and also keep your weight left. Then it's simply a matter of throwing the club as quickly as possible, and earlier in the sequence, than you would for a chip shot or a full swing.

I find that most players are able to quickly grasp the idea of moving the circles in the right order on short shots with small movements, but they start to get a little panicky when they get to a full shot. It's all happening faster and bigger, and there doesn't seem to be enough time to process everything that has to happen for the swing to come off the right way.

One thing that really seems to help impart the feeling and understanding of good sequencing is the use of a training aid that makes it easier to feel where the clubhead is. One device I really like is the Orange Whip, designed by PGA professional Jim Hackenberg. The Orange Whip has a flexible shaft and a heavy rubber ball on the clubhead end, along with some weight built into the butt end of the club. When you swing it, the shaft flex causes you to load the heavy head at the top of the backswing and unload it in the right order—otherwise you can't support the stress of the heavier weight in transition and you fall into an awkward position. Making five or six swings with the Whip automatically prompts you to change your sequencing to get the heavy head to unload down by the ball—not too early or too late in the downswing. The heavy ball forces you to turn your body to help support the weight in the backswing, and it even helps you stretch out your muscles at the same time. The trick is to make the swings with the ball in place and feel the flexible shaft unload the weight through impact and equate the same feel to the clubhead on a real metal shaft. The principle is the same—you just have to believe that it still holds true. Then it's a matter of letting physics work for you.

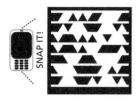

SNAP IT!

The weighted Orange Whip training device has a heavy ball on the end instead of a clubhead and a flexible shaft designed to help you feel the loading and unloading of energy (1). When you make a good backswing, you support the weight of the head to the top with a good body turn (2), then sequence the motion on the downswing so that the head unloads and whips through right where the ball would be (3). If you unload the head too soon (4), the weighted head pulls you into an awkward position you can feel right away, and pulls you out of balance in the finish (5).

# CHAPTER 3

# CONTROLLING THE CLUBFACE

· · · · · · · · · · · · · · · · · · · · · · · · · · · · · · · · · · · · · · · · · · · · ·

Spend any time with Bob Vokey, Titleist's longtime wedge designer, and you'll hear him talk about the old days. Back then, he says, guys hit the ball through "windows." That's Bob's way of saying that players used to work the ball a lot more than they do now. If you imagine a twelve-pane window, with four squares across and four squares top to bottom, the old-timers could pick any of the panes and hit it through the one they'd called. The new guys, he says, can only hit it through three.

I've spent time around lots of talented junior and college players, and that's not very far from the truth. I've seen a lot of highly skilled players, but many of them play as if they have only one gear. If they're on, they shoot a really low number. But if they're off, they shoot 82. I want to tell them that when they start having one of those off days, they just need to simplify things, pick a three-quarter-speed shot that goes out there 240 yards, find the ball, and hit it up there in the middle of the green. Then they'd have something—something Jack Nicklaus used to win a million golf tournaments and all those majors. He played with what he found at the range that day, and he understood how to control his ball and control his game. My career obviously isn't in the same universe as Jack's—whose is?—but I had plenty of days where I turned a 77 into a 71 by managing my short game and hitting shots I knew I could control.

What does that mean for you? You might be thinking you'd be happy to be able to pick one of those panes and shake it through that one more often that not. Being able to hit one shot consistently is definitely a positive step in your game, but it's not the final step. The good news is that if you can digest the basics of form and sequence that we've been talking about in the last two chapters, you can be a lot more consistent. And you'll also have all the tools you need to take more control of your overall game, from tee to green. When you know the hows and whys of hitting a low chip versus a lofted pitch, you start to tune in to the feel and sequencing that will serve you on full shots from the fairway and off the tee. As you'll soon see, the sequencing rules for all of those shots are the same. The only difference is the speed at which they happen.

Whenever I give a short-game clinic and start talking about using the wrists and forearms and controlling trajectory, I see a lot of the average players get a worried look. They think there's some kind of complicated magic involved—a set of skills that are difficult to learn. When I show the players in those clinics the three basic varieties of shots—low, medium and high—and the change in wrist movement for the three, they try it and comment that they can't believe it's that easy. My response is that you couldn't possibly say anything nicer to me. My goal here is to show you how to use your wrists and hands, and to get you to understand that what at first may seem "out of control" will actually reduce the number of moving parts in your swing. It's a simpler way to add to your arsenal of shots, and a simpler way to control the ball.

It all starts with the left wrist.

If you set your grip the way we talked about in the first chapter, you've established a hold on the club that allows the back of your left wrist to equate to the clubface. If that's the case, whatever you do with your left wrist at the setup or during the swing will impact the ball.

To really make the connection, get yourself a Ping-Pong paddle. If you hold the paddle in your regular golf grip using your left hand, the face should be completely vertical when you have the paddle out in front of you. Make a series of slow one-handed swings with the paddle, first without any extra movement of your wrist. If you keep the back of your left wrist in the same position that it's in at setup throughout the swing, the ball will come straight off the face with what I would call "standard" loft. Now make some slow swings where you turn your left wrist "down," or toward the ball, through impact. This reduces loft and produces a lower shot. If you make some slow swings and "hold off" the paddle—that is, you delay your wrist turn so that the face of the paddle stays facing toward the sky—you're adding loft and hitting a higher shot.

In your short game, using a hook spin and slice spin to cause the ball to roll out more or check up is the next level of sophistication beyond controlling the amount of loft on the face. When I hit a low-running chip shot, I consciously swing the toe of the club through impact a little bit sooner than the heel—in addition to turning my left wrist down to reduce the loft on the club—to produce some hook spin on the ball. That spin causes the ball to land, bounce lower initially, and hug the ground sooner, all qualities that produce a longer roll out. My first teacher, Mr. Lanning, pointed out that even though I might be

When I turn my right wrist down, toward the ball, the face of the paddle points toward the ground (1). If I swing through while holding the face open (2), pointing at the sky, the paddle angles upward. You can see a dramatic difference in the positioning of my wrist.

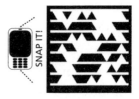

chipping with a lofted club, the less backspin I put on the ball, the better chance I would have of predicting what my shot would do on the first bounce. It is this ability to predict and control how the ball reacts that will allow you to have a great short game, and why I play low- and medium-height run-out shots so often.

When you're faced with a tier situation—where you're on one level and the flag is on a flat shelf above or below you—the best play may be to fly the ball to the same tier as the flag. When there isn't much room on the tier, you can certainly do the opposite of what I just described for a run-out shot. Swinging through with the heel slightly ahead of the toe will pop the ball up in the air and add more backspin, two things that will cause the ball to land softly with less roll out. But I don't hit that shot very often, if at all. I prefer to hit my lofted pitch shot—which I'll go into more detail in Chapter 6—and rely on the loft of the shot to get the ball to stop. Swinging the heel through impact first brings in too many variables—most of them bad—for my taste.

By combining varying degrees of wrist movement and some subtle changes to your setup position, you can create a tremendous variety of different trajectories on any shot—from a chip to a full-iron shot from the fairway. Using the paddle, go to your address position again. Now bend the back of your left wrist slightly so that the fingers on your left hand are angled more toward the target. Notice how you can immediately see more of the face of the paddle. By making this backward shift in your setup, you're increasing the loft on the club, and exposing more of the bottom of the club to the ground. This is exactly what I described as the fundamental setup position for a bunker shot or a lofted pitch. On any shot, if you play your hands back, away from the target, and angle the shaft backward versus straight up and down, you increase the effective loft of the club. The opposite is obviously true if you move your hand toward the target at address in a forward press. This reduces the effective loft of the club.

The next step is to experiment with some of these different address positions and wrist movements to get a feel for how much of one or the other impacts the actual ball flight. Before you go out and swing away at full speed, try this sequence of drills to familiarize yourself with what I've been talking about.

Standing just off the green, dump out a small bucket of practice balls. Now, while holding the club in just your left-handed grip, practice hitting small, low pitch shots while turning the left wrist "down" through impact. If you've ever played tennis, it should feel like you're hitting a topspin backhand. Another good description of the feel I've heard is that it's like throwing a Frisbee.

It's perfectly okay to hit a few grounders and skulls at the start—it takes a few minutes to register and master the feel I'm talking about here. I had LPGA player Amanda Blumenherst try this drill near the beginning of our work and she had difficulty because she was tugging on the handle. Once she got the feel of turning her wrist down and letting the rotation of her forearm provide the speed for the low shot, she got better quickly.

Once you're consistently making crisp contact, simply add your right hand to the club and start adding some lower-body pivot to the move. All of a sudden, you've got a reliable little shot to hit around the green that's pretty much impervious to bad lies, pressure, or any other problems you might run into. Just remember to let that left-wrist turn-down control the motion. Don't yank the grip back and forth.

After hitting a small bucket of shots left-handed, gather the balls up and bring them back to a spot just off the green. Now hold the club in your right hand, just off the grip and on the steel of the shaft. Start in an upright position, with your right hand waist-high, and practice driving an imaginary nail into the wall in front of you. Once you've done that a few times, turn your arm over so that the imaginary nail is going into a wall to your side. If you're doing it correctly, the grip of the club should be arcing back and forth under your forearm. Now, bend over and brush the grass as you do this, letting the bounce of the club skip along the ground.

Make some tiny swings without the ball at first, feeling as though you're skipping a rock along the top of the water, then try to hit some shots one-handed, really throwing the clubhead early in the downswing. Just like with the left-handed shot, you might struggle with solid contact at first. But when you get the bounce skipping along the ground, you'll start to produce some nice, high, soft shots. You've just re-created a bunker shot and a lofted pitch. Add your left hand to the club (without restricting the sideways throwing move) and let your arms make the swing. Now you've got three windows for your shots.

As you can imagine, it's far, far easier to have a sense for what is happening at impact when you're talking about a 10-yard chip or a 20-yard pitch. You can actually see and feel what your wrists are doing during that motion—something you can't do as easily when you're hitting a 6-iron from the fairway.

But one of the exciting parts about this information is that it's just as applicable to full shots, even if you can't fully feel what's happening at the moment of truth. If you practice turning your left wrist down on a 10-yard chip shot, you're developing a feel that is directly applicable to a 7-iron shot from the fairway. Replicate the move and feel on a full-iron shot and you'll start to see a difference in trajectory on shots where you turn it down. Are you going to be able to have the ball on a string from day one, zipping it in high or low on command? No,

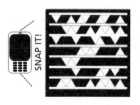

To reinforce the connection between your wrist movement and the loft on the clubface, practice hitting two different kinds of one-handed shots. First, turn your left wrist down and hit short, low one-handed bump and runs (1). Then switch to your right hand and let the clubhead swing through and release on a high shot (2).

but you'll be gaining confidence and control every day, and your creativity level will increase in lockstep with your ability to hit the ball higher or lower. Even if you can't hit the seventh window versus the tenth one with perfect accuracy, being able to hit a shot with a relatively lower trajectory—even if it isn't specific or perfect—is way, way better than being confronted with a strong headwind, shrugging your shoulders and hitting your plain-vanilla shot, and hoping for the best.

One clubface control question I get a lot is about producing

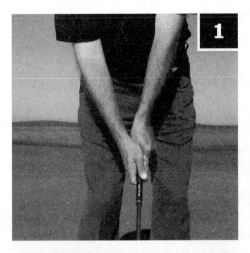

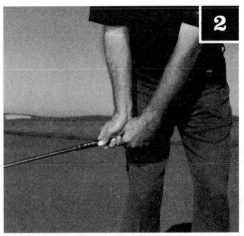

These photographs isolate how wrist action in a simple pitch shot determines loft. From address (1), I make a waist-high backswing hinging the wrists, with a slight bow of my left wrist (2). In the finish, the club stays low and moves around my body, waist-high as I pivot (3).

backspin. I'm sure you've seen tour players hit a little 30-yard low pitch that hits the green, hops once and zips to a stop right next to the hole. That's a cool trick, and a great display of talent—and that's the problem I have with the shot. You've got to be super precise in how you make contact with the ball, and very sharp in how you aim. Catch it just a little bit heavy and that shot ends up 40 feet short of the hole. Catch it thin and you're over the green looking at a bogey.

When I started working with Sergio Garcia, I saw a guy with

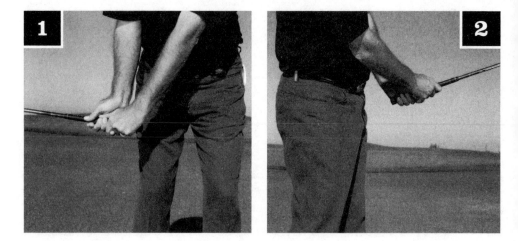

Compare this backswing picture (1) with the low shot—the club is hinged more and the knuckles of the left wrist are pointing more upward. The club moves more upward in the finish (2), a sign that the grip end hasn't moved as much through impact.

an absolutely tremendous set of hands. He could dial that little zip pitch in two or three feet from the hole on command. Except when he couldn't. The problem for him was that he could hit it tight eight times out of ten and have a real chance at birdie, but the two times he hit a poor shot he made bogey, not par. Compounding the problem was that he never seemed to play the simplest shot that would solve the problem. It's not that he didn't have the talent, obviously. He had just never learned a more basic pitch shot that relied less on precise timing.

I taught Sergio how to hit a plain-vanilla pitch shot using the bounce on the bottom of the club—a shot with not very much backspin that rolled out like a putt. Under straightforward conditions—an open green in front of him and no tiers to contend with—he quickly got good enough with the plain shot to hit it in a three-foot window every time. Even his bad shots

For a super-high shot, the address position changes. My stance is wider and I bend my left wrist and set the shaft so that it angles slightly away from the hole (1). The backswing is much larger, with more wrist hinge (2). The knuckles on the left hand point straight back from the target. The club returns to impact with the same backward shaft lean (3), with the wrists already unhinging past the point they started at address. The shot requires more speed and a bigger swing, and the corresponding finish position has more shoulder turn, a vertical shaft and the club moved all the way around the body (4).

From up the line, you can see that I'm hitting three different shots with pretty similar body movement. The major difference between a low (1), medium (2), and high (3) shot is the movement of my wrists and when the clubhead releases relative to the body. On the low shot, my right wrist is turning the club down and my hands are holding the shaft in a forward shaft angle—leaning toward the target. As my hands move less in relation to my body, the clubhead passes the hands and moves around with more loft earlier in the swing. My hands are in the same position in pictures 2 and 3, but I threw the clubhead much more aggressively—and earlier—in the super high shot in picture 3.

were still in a very makeable position. Plus, he still had the zip pitch for when he needed to get to a tight pin on a tier. The moral of that story is that just because you can hit one shot really well—even at tour level—doesn't mean you don't need to know a few different shots. When I played on tour, I didn't have Sergio's talent for the long game, so I needed to exploit every advantage I could.

What does this mean for you? One thing it *doesn't* mean is that you keep trying to move the ball back in your stance and chop down on it to try to make the ball spin, either from the fairway or on a short-game shot. Gouging a big hole in the ground doesn't have any impact on backspin—only hitting the ball first before you hit the ground, and having enough speed through impact, produces it. I would actually argue that backspin is something you don't even need to be thinking much about on any of your short-game shots and most of your long-game shots. It's really only a factor if you're one of the few players who swings faster than 115 miles per hour or so with the driver. I'm not in that group, and I know most of you aren't, either.

I would say that if you can learn the basic low and high chips and pitches I teach here and have the super-high lofted pitch shot in your pocket for emergencies, you don't have to even worry about backspin. Go and pick a ball that gives you the optimum mix of qualities you like off the tee and from the fairway and let your technique provide distance control around the green.

# Chapter 4

# SEQUENCING YOUR GAME

. . . . . . . . . . . . . . . . . . . . . . . . . . . . . . . . . . . . . . . . . . . . . . .

We've talked a lot about sequencing the actual act of swinging the club, but the physical part of the game isn't the only place where sequencing is important. I like to think of a day of golf—whether it's a simple practice session, a casual round, or a tournament match for the club championship— as a process. And like any process, defining the goal and the steps toward meeting the goal is standard procedure.

If you don't change a single thing about your physical golf swing after reading this book and watching the videos that come with it, you'll still get better if I can get you to recognize one thing I learned—the hard way—in almost thirty years as a tour player and teacher. Golf is about learning to ask yourself the right questions, and then having the discipline to pick one answer, commit to it, and let it fly.

Think about it. You've got an extended period of time to walk or ride between your shots. You can watch the scenery, think about your swing, burn up over a mistake you made on the last hole, laugh at a joke your friend tells, drink a beverage, or do a hundred other things that may or may not be related to hitting good shots. When you get to your ball, you have to organize all those thoughts and pick something out of there that is going to make the ball go somewhere positive. Then you need all the thoughts to quiet down so that you can shift into "athletic" mode, where you actually have to physically perform the shot.

Golf isn't like baseball or tennis, where so much of what you do is in reaction to what somebody else is trying to do to you. The ball is sitting there, and you need to impose your strategy—your sequence—on it. It's a unique game, and a unique mix of social and solitary. I've had some lonely rounds, even when I was playing in front of five thousand people in a gallery.

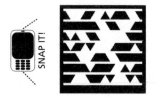

If you want to gain more control over your game, you need to come up with an organizing structure around it. Think of the day as a sequence of events, and picture the events within that master list as having their own individual processes that make them efficient. Let's break that down broadly into three categories: the pre-round routine, the pre-shot routine, and the practice routine.

## PRE-ROUND ROUTINE

The first thing you think about when you hear the term "pre-round routine" is probably the balls you hit and practice putting you do in advance of your round. These are certainly an important part of the routine—and I'm going to cover what my process is for those in a second—but your routine actually starts before you even get the clubs out of the trunk of your car.

In the lead-up to a round of golf, you have a certain set of expectations and hopes for the day. They might not be anything that you write out specifically in a list, but they're there. You might be looking forward to getting outside and having a good time with some friends you haven't seen in a while. You might be trying to make a business connection with a client. You could be playing a qualifying round for the third flight at your club championship. Or maybe you're getting out by yourself to hit some shots and play two balls just for the joy of the game.

What I'm suggesting is that you define for yourself what your specific goals and expectations are for the day as you're driving to the course—whether they're something concrete golfwise, like a score, a certain number of birdies or pars or bogeys, or a certain number of really solid shots; a concrete business or client goal; or something "softer," like enjoying your time with a friend, making the most of the good weather, or taking in the scenery as you walk the cliffside holes at Pebble Beach. Forming specific—and realistic—expectations has plenty of benefits. If you're getting ready to play in a pressure situation like a tournament or a match, you can diffuse some of the pressure by hooking your expectations to something other than a finish on the leaderboard or an outcome in a match. Maybe it's hitting five tee shots exactly the way you planned to, or beating your own target score. It's a strategy that Jack Nicklaus used throughout his major championship career. He wasn't thinking about Tom Watson or Lee Trevino or Arnold Palmer on Sunday as much as he was thinking about the score that he thought he'd need to shoot. If he shot the number (or better), he was handling the only part of the scenario that he could control.

The process of asking yourself questions also starts on the

way to the course. When you start to think about your hopes and expectations, you need to ask yourself if the conditions surrounding your game make those expectations and hopes possible. Weather is a great example here. Some players are so put off by wind and wet that they can't enjoy the game under those conditions. It's nothing to be ashamed of, but it's something you need to understand about yourself before you psych yourself up to shoot a career score in a late October qualifying round when it's 52 degrees and wet, or when you commit to a week in Ireland playing thirty-six a day with your buddies. Tom Watson won a lot of tournaments where he relished the idea of testing himself against rough weather to see how well he could perform when his grips were damp and the wind was howling. That was a matter of him pegging his goals and expectations toward a realistic assessment of the conditions and recalibrating what a great score would be given those conditions. Then he went out and competed with himself against that score.

I like to set goals and expectations for myself so I can measure my progress by something other than the score on the card—which can be influenced by a lot of fluky things. I might hit the ball poorly but putt out of my mind and shoot 71, which would be a really good score under the circumstances. I might shoot that same 71 after hitting fifteen greens, which could be a terrible score given what might have happened. I go into each round committed to following my "See It, Feel It, Trust It" routine—which I describe below—for every shot. I grade myself on how successful I am at following that routine during my round. If I followed my routine and was fully committed to sixty-five shots out of seventy-two, I pair that score with my actual score, the number of fairways I hit, the number of greens I hit, and the number of putts I took to get a comprehensive review of how I did.

Once you've set your expectations and goals for your round,

you want to be able to get to the course and prepare yourself in the most efficient way. I see plenty of my amateur pro-am partners out on the range early, looking for a mechanical tip that can help fix a crooked ball flight. If they insist, I'll give them a Band-Aid to try to help them through—after all, they paid good money to play with me—but my preference would be to help them get into a mode where they get an idea of the kind of game they brought with them that day and then try to maximize that.

That's a fancy way of saying that your pre-round time should be spent stretching out and getting ready to hit *your* shots on the holes you're going to play, not looking for a new kind of shot to hit. You can be the 20-handicapper who hits a 30-yard slice, but if you warm up and get an accurate visual on your ball flight, you can walk to the first tee, set up for that slice, and end up in the fairway.

I get ready for a tournament round by starting with a few putts. If I'm early and have extra time, I'll hang out at the putting green. Next I'll go to the range and start with some short pitch shots. I'm just trying to get the feel in my hands and arms and stretch out a little. I work my way through the bag for twenty to thirty minutes before finishing with the club I'm going to hit off the first tee. I hit six or seven balls with that club—usually the driver or a 3-wood—then go to the practice bunker and spend five or ten minutes getting a feel for the sand conditions. When I have fifteen minutes left to go before my tee time, I go to the practice green and hit a variety of 20-footers first, to start to dial in my feel for distance. Then I finish up with a series of short 18-inch putts to reinforce the feeling of success—the ball going in the hole.

I'm not trying to fix anything or make any big mechanical changes to my swing during this pre-round process. It's entirely designed to get me stretched out and warm, and to latch on to a swing thought for the day that promotes my sense of feel for each shot. I might know that I'm stiff and not turning as well, or that my long irons just aren't that crisp. Having that information helps me make some strategic decisions when I'm out on the course. You might sense that your lag-putting touch just isn't dialed-in. That fact could cause you to adjust your expectations for the day, and change your focus to another goal—hitting fairways, maybe.

The point here is to help you start making some conscious decisions and assessments about your game before you play a round instead of getting out of your car, walking to the first tee, and hoping for the best. If your goal is to shoot consistently lower scores, that prep time can help make it happen, even if you don't make a single mechanical change to your swing.

When I was a junior player, I used to practice for hours just hitting ball after ball in the hole from 18 inches away to get built-in a feeling of success. Now it's how I finish my pre-round routine to go to the tee in a positive frame of mind.

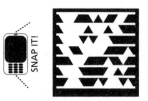

# PRE-SHOT ROUTINE

When it comes to your pre-shot routine, the goal is to ask yourself the right questions about the shot scenario you're facing, then use the same routine time after time to incorporate the answer into the swing you make. The big-picture way that I do that for a tee shot, a shot from the fairway, a short-game shot and a putt is the same, but the individual parts for the different kinds of shots change depending on the kind of information I need.

Let's start with a putt. Reading greens is a big topic, and one I've covered in-depth in *The Art of Putting* and *The Art of Scoring*, but I'll give a short summary here in case you don't have access to those two books. For any courses that I play regularly—like the two here at Grayhawk in Scottsdale, where I teach, or for PGA Tour tournament venues—I use a detailed book on each green and its contours. I make notes of the prevailing tilt of each green, the direction of the grain, and the location of the prominent tiers and other landmarks like ridges or valleys. I let my eyes—and feet—make the read, but the book gives me details that help me make a decision for my approach shots as well as my putts.

If I'm playing a course for the first time, I have to rely on my eyes and feet. That means I'm watching my shots from the fairway and my short-game shots as they roll onto the putting surface to see how they react. As I walk up to the green, or walk from the cart to the green, I'm looking to see the prevailing tilt of the green—the angle at which the course architect designed the green so that water doesn't stand on the putting surface. If you can find the low point around the green—and there's often an actual physical drain there—you'll immediately have the basis for the default direction that putts on that green will break.

Once you have that big-picture information, you can then make the specific read for the putt you're facing. First, look for the break from behind your ball, then walk behind the hole and look for it from that direction. When you return to your ball from behind the hole, make sure to walk to the ball on the low side—opposite from the direction the ball will break—and look at the putt from a spot halfway between the hole and your ball. If the putt breaks from left to right, you want to walk to the right side of the hole and read the putt from the halfway point. From those three spots you can gain the most useful information about what the putt actually does.

Once you've picked the apex point of your putt—the place where the ball starts to curve toward the hole—the first critical part of your pre-putt routine kicks in. You need to be able to line yourself up so that you're aimed at this apex point—not the hole. It's extremely common for players to go through all of the process of making a read, then step up to the ball and subconsciously cheat their aim more toward the hole, because that's what they're looking at. Then they use their stroke to try to push or pull the ball to the apex point. That isn't a consistent way to putt—and that, coupled with underestimating how much the ball will break, is the main reason that people miss putts on the low side.

When you've picked your aiming point, you want to have a routine that puts you in position to hit the ball on the line that you picked during your read. Walk up to the ball with the putter in your right hand. Stand so your feet are perpendicular to your start line, turn your head to look where you want the ball to start, and then set the putterhead behind the ball. I believe this is the most reliable way to aim the putter. Once the putter is in place, use the clubhead as the reference point to get settled into your putting stance.

Once you're in your stance, the time for wondering if you have the right line is over. At this point you need to visualize the roll of the putt in your mind, plug in a specific swing

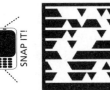

SNAP IT!

Start your pre-putt routine from behind the ball (1), visualizing your line with both eyes looking at the target. Move into your stance holding the putter in your right hand (2), and set the putter behind the ball aligned to your target (3). Once you've aimed the face, align the rest of your body to the putter (4), take one last look at the target and let the stroke go (5). Your goal is to try to roll the ball squarely off the putter face (6).

thought, and then pull the trigger. Your conscious thought at this point is to try to roll the ball squarely off the putterface. If you have rolled the ball smoothly and squarely off the putterface with the appropriate speed and on the line you've picked, you've done your job.

Is it as easy as that? Yes and no.

Putting is not as complicated as many people make it. But there is a definite strategy and process to being able to clear your mind like that and let it go. That process flows hand-in-hand with the read and the pre-putt routine. I worked with Dr. David Cook, a sports psychologist, for many years, and he helped me develop a routine called "See It, Feel It, Trust It." The purpose of that routine was to have a psychological and physical checklist to run through that emphasized the process of thinking about and hitting the shot, not the outcome of it. By going down the checklist, I did everything that was in my power to make a good read and a good stroke. Once the ball leaves the putter, the rest is out of my hands.

Becoming more process-oriented versus results-oriented gives you a better chance to handle pressure situations. If you're thinking about the checklist and the process you need to go through, you're distracted from worrying about what happens if you miss. I had the chance to ask Stewart Cink about the birdie putt he made on the 72nd hole when he won the British Open in 2009. I really wanted to know how he made the change from his belly putter back to a standard-length putter. He told me that even though he'd had great success with the belly putter, he simply decided to use a standard putter again. The main thing he worked on with his teacher when making the change was not mechanics but process. He told me that on that final putt, all he did was go through his process just as he had practiced, and that it really did help him avoid getting distracted by the enormity of the situation. This is a great lesson for all of us.

Real life will certainly find a way to intrude—we're not robots—but every little bit helps. Having a process also helps you handle the inevitable peaks and valleys in your game. If you know you're following your plan and making good reads, you won't get as upset when you go through a stretch where the ball just isn't going in. It gives you a basis for going back and checking your fundamentals, and for giving yourself a pass if you're making good strokes. Sometimes the ball just doesn't fall.

My checklist incorporated parts of the pre-putt routine I just described, along with some psychological techniques designed to clear my head of clutter at the most important time. After surveying my situation and picking out the shot I wanted to hit, I would get into my stance as I described and make a practice stroke. But the practice stroke wasn't mindless. I would "See It," meaning I would actually visualize the path of the ball from where I was standing into the hole. It is important to go through this visualizing step on every putt—whether it's 3 feet or 30.

Once I had the visualization down, I would pick one of the particular swing thoughts or feels I was working with for that round and plug it in, to "Feel It." I'm going to tell you more about those feels and how to use them in the next chapter, but one example might be as simple as keeping the right elbow soft. Having that individual feel plugged in is an enormous help, because it acts like the tuner on your radio. When you have the strong local station tuned in, you aren't hearing the static and chatter from the other weaker stations on the dial.

After I visualize the line and plug in the feel during my practice stroke, the next step is to let it go, to "Trust It." There isn't a player alive who hasn't stood over a shot and gotten last-second anxiety about aim or line or mechanics or the pressure of the situation. When you decide to trust it, you're giving the decision-making part of the process its own place, but you're refusing to let it leak out of its own spot on that checklist. Let the shot go and pay attention to the feedback—the quality of your contact, where the ball went in comparison with your read—so you can make the proper adjustments on the next shot.

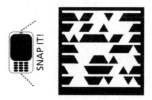

I've talked about See It, Feel It, Trust It in the context of putting and short-game shots, but it's a process I've used for more than twenty years on every shot I hit. The parameters of a tee shot or a 7-iron from the fairway are obviously different than a 10-foot putt or a bunker shot, but you can use the same framework.

Picking a shot from the tee, from the fairway, and from around the green is very much like setting up shots in a game of pool. From the tee, you want to pick the shot that is the best combination of distance and reliability. That's obviously a sliding scale depending on the situation, the design of the hole, your handicap level, and how you're hitting the ball on that given day. Many times, a driver isn't the right choice, because the advantage of 20 more yards compared with your 3-wood is more than offset by all the trouble that comes into play if you hit the ball off line. I like to tell my amateur pro-am partners to try to put themselves in a position to hit shots they like to hit. I don't care if a par-5 is 600 yards long. If you're not hitting your driver well, you're better off hitting a hybrid off the tee, another hybrid to lay up, a third hybrid up in front of the green and taking your chances getting up and down to save par. You have a much better chance of making bogey that way than if you're reloading and hitting three off the tee because your tee shot went out of bounds.

When I'm hitting a full shot, I do the same visualization as I would for a putt. I see the ball flight from where I'm hitting to where the shot lands, and imagine how the ball will run out after it hits. It's just that the information gathering and question asking that goes before it is more comprehensive. On a putt, you're making a read based on the contours of the green and the grain of the grass. On a full shot, you're processing a lot more variables. What's the wind doing? Is it hot outside? Humid? Are you hitting to an elevated target? Are the greens firm and bouncy, or soft and receptive? Are you hitting shots with a prevailing curve, left to right or right to left? Where are the most dangerous places to miss—hazards, deep grass, the short side of the green—and how do I make sure to avoid them? The game becomes more three-dimensional, and you have a lot more shot choices.

Around the green, you're making a lot of the same three-dimensional decisions you have for a full shot. On greenside shots, I check the quality of my lie, then step off the total distance to the hole and the distance to where I want the ball to land. How do I choose a landing spot on a short-game shot? I want my shots to get on the green as soon as possible after they've carried any potential obstacles that would make it difficult for the ball to run out like a putt. In other words, I want to carry the rough and the fringe, and any significant ridges or tiers, and land the ball where it can roll to the hole. Then I pick the appropriate low-running or lofted chip shot to replicate the trajectory I'm visualizing. I'm going to talk about the five basic shots you need in your arsenal in Chapter 6.

Once I've surveyed my lie and visualized the shot I need to hit my landing spot and roll to the hole, I go through my pre-shot and See It, Feel It, Trust It routine, just as I would for a full shot or a putt, and commit to the strategy decision I've made. I'm convinced that average amateur players would significantly lower their handicaps if they simply committed to the shot they were going to hit—even if it was the wrong one for the situation—instead of hitting the right shot halfheartedly. How many times have you been unsure about what to do, and then made a tentative stab at a chip shot and stubbed it, leaving it in the grass? If you don't feel good about your short game, or you're feeling the pressure, just take your hybrid and set up the ball like a putt. Make a big putting stroke with the hybrid and the ball will shoot up out of the grass and get rolling quickly. With some practice, you can get good at judging how that shot will roll on fairway grass and through the fringe, and you can run it up there 5 or 10 feet from the hole, where you have a chance to make the putt. If that's the shot you feel the best about hitting, go with it.

My 20-handicap friends ask me all the time how I can expect them to make strategy decisions about places to hit it or not hit it when they can't control their ball like a tour player can. "If it was as easy as telling myself not to hit it short and right, I'd just tell myself to hit in the middle of the green and do that." I get that, but as you've probably heard Bob Rotella say, golf isn't a game of perfect. Nobody can execute a shot every single time. Not even tour players. But tour players have a plan for every hole they play and almost every shot they hit. My view is that having a plan is better than not having one and just whacking away at it and hoping for the best.

I want you to approach each hole you play with a strategy and see the specific shot you want to hit, even if you don't always pull it off. When you make a technical mistake and put a bad swing on it, you can accept it as something that happens from time to time, then start the strategic decision-making process again on the next shot. If you don't have that vision for

Picking the right shot for the situation has to incorporate hitting a shot you're comfortable with. Practice hitting a hybrid from off the green using your putting stroke and you'll have a pressure-proof default bump and run shot to use on a tight lie or when you aren't feeling confident with your pitching game.

SNAP IT!

what your easiest route to the hole is, you're making life much harder for yourself, because you might hit a technically perfect shot but end up in a terrible spot because it was the wrong shot for the situation. I want to see good decisions and good swings get rewarded. The only way to do that is to have a plan.

## PRACTICE ROUTINE

What sometimes gets lost in all the talk about pre-round and pre-shot routines is the importance of structured practice. I'm sure you've gone out and pounded a large bucket of balls, hitting driver after driver. That's great, and sometimes I do the exact same thing. But if you aren't working on something specific and aiming at a specific target when you hit those balls, you aren't getting any benefit out of the practice routine except for the calories you burn. The same is true on the practice green. Standing over the same 10-footer and rolling putt after putt just proves that you can make that particular 10-footer. You're grooving a stroke for one putt, when you need to be tuning your feel to hit a variety of different putts.

When I work with tour players on their short game, I start with an "analysis" session in which I make an assessment of the parts of the player's game that he or she is interested in improving. Once I've done that, we start taking some steps to improve, and work on no more than one or two concepts in a given session. I'll see the player for an extended session in Scottsdale or on a Tuesday at a tour event and leave him or her with a concrete practice plan for when I'm not there to watch. The player then has a specific program that he or she can plug into the practice-day routine just for short-game shots or putting—doing specific drills and routines to work on a specific skill. Even at the tour level, I see lots of players who equate activity with progress. They believe that if they're out there hitting balls—even if it's without a plan or some objective way to determine if they're getting better—they're putting in the work. Without that structure or measuring stick, it's mostly just exercise.

I can appreciate the fact that we're all busy with work and family and real life, and sometimes one 18-hole round a week early on Saturday morning is all you have time to play. That only reinforces the idea that if you do find some time to work on your game, you should get the most out of that time with a specific plan. In Chapter 9, I'm going to show you how you can get your total game in sequence with a month of twenty-minute practice sessions. All you have to do is carve out the time.

# Chapter 5

# THE BOOK OF FEELS

. . . . . . . . . . . . . . . . . . . . . . . . . . . . . . . . . . . . . . . . . . . . .

One of the standard clichés in the golf teaching business is "feel vs. real." Of course, there's a reason that clichés become clichés—there's a lot of truth to them. One of the first things I do when you and I have our first lesson is to watch what you do in your short game or with your putting and then ask you what your intention is. The goal is to get the intention to match the execution.

My goal in any lesson I give—and in this book—is to give you the mechanics and the thought process you need to decide which shot you want to hit, and then to match the shot you've visualized to the one you hit. And, just as importantly, to understand how and why you did or didn't pull it off.

That matching process is where the concept of "feel vs. real" comes in. I can't walk out onto a golf course and play "blank"— in other words, just mindlessly execute a series of movements to produce a shot. Even if I could do it, I wouldn't want to. To me, one of the main reasons this game is so engaging is the con-stant—and constantly changing—series of mental and physical challenges it presents over the course of eighteen holes. Solving the puzzle is what makes it fun.

If you're determined to play "conscious" golf, where you take in experiences and information and advice and apply it to your game to solve the puzzle, you need to be able to recognize how your body feels and the state of your game from day to day. As I've said before, people aren't machines. The mechanical advice I gave you in a lesson might get you hitting good shots for a week or a month, but for the lesson to really "take," you have to be able to recognize when things start to get off and to find the swing thought or feel that adjusts the dial and refocuses the picture.

As you work on the things we've talked about in this book, you're going to connect more strongly with some of the concepts and "feels" than others. You might be a visual person who needs to see pictures or video so you can copy some part of the movement to get it down. Many times during a lesson, I'll reach in and swing the putter or the wedge for the student while they are holding the club. Or maybe you read how I describe one of the feels I have during a swing and the description clicks, and repeating it to yourself during your swing helps you.

I've been playing for more than thirty years, and I'm always cycling to the different swing thoughts and feels that I've banked over the years. The one or two I pick for a given day click in based on how my body feels, the way I'm swinging the club, and the issues I'm dealing with in my game that day.

I want to emphasize that the swing thoughts and feels I'm talking about here aren't designed to get you to move the club any differently. They're all designed to get you closer to your ideal swing or putting stroke. They're all individual triggers that should help get you closer to your template.

For example, I know that when I get in a pressure situation, my lower body tends to stop rotating through on the downswing. The result is that my arms get too active, and I end up hitting a pull or a hook. If I'm playing on Sunday afternoon trying to win a tournament, my swing thought or feel might be "rotate hips hard." But I've been in situations where I plugged in that swing thought and it didn't help. I needed to find something else to think about. On other days, I had a good response from using the feeling of my hands dropping from their own weight as the first move of my downswing. Both thoughts are designed to prompt the same thing—to get me back to my perfect swing.

Before you start to worry that the feel you pick for your next round is the right one, remember this: Whatever feel you pick, just having a simple thought or two to focus on during your swing or putting stroke is better for your game than playing blank. When you commit to having just one or two thoughts it provides a valuable filter for your head. It just isn't productive to stand over the ball thinking about a million different basic mechanical movements. The swing happens so fast, even on a putt, that you can't physically control it to that degree, and trying to do so just gets in the way. Clicking in a single thought (or two at the most) clears your head and prompts you to move in sequence.

In the sections below, I'm going to go through some of the swing thoughts and feels that have worked for me and that prompt the kind of swings I think are the most efficient. I'll say right up front that all of them might not work for you, and that's perfectly okay. My goal for you is to identify the feels that work. I want you to catalog these feels and, more specifically, what they do for your game. That's an important step, because some of them might provoke a result that's "bad" under neutral conditions but could be something you need under other circumstances. For example, locking in on the feel of the right elbow straightening and the forearms rotating on your putting stroke might cause you to pull putts. That's obviously not what you want, but cataloging that feel gives you something to plug in on a day when you're struggling with pushing putts out to the right. In other words, it might be the right pull on a different day.

A good habit to get into on every round you play (and in life in general) is to remember the good stuff. It's easy to look back on the day and think about the shot you hit out of bounds on 17 or the approach shot you dumped into the creek on 8, but it's far, far more productive to keep track of the shots you hit exactly the way you wanted. Mark it right on your scorecard— the shots you liked, and what you were feeling as you made them. You'll start to build a library of how you were feeling physically and about your game, and what feels seemed to click under those circumstances. It's certainly not an exact science, but even a small bit of help is better than walking out there with nothing but fourteen clubs and a prayer. When you walk off the green after shooting 106, you can stew about it and tell yourself that you just played bad, or you can look for the common threads and start to sort them.

## PUTTING FEELS

The basic idea of loading and unloading the putterhead during the stroke is a new one for a lot of people. Before we even get to describing some of the other feels and swing thoughts you could use in your stroke, I want to give you a way to connect the motion in the stroke with another sports movement.

Believe it or not, the way the right wrist moves in a putting stroke (for a right-handed player) is very much like the wrist movement in shooting a basketball. Instead of "freezing" your wrists and arms and using a stiff upper body turn to hit the ball, I want you to use your hands. You can generate more energy on the putterhead with far less effort and a smaller movement, and relying on gravity and physics to send the ball on its line is much more consistent than getting rigid and overcontrolling.

When you shoot a basketball, your shooting arm is vertical, and the wrist provides the motion for the ball to leave the hand by moving directly in line with the arm. To get that feel, simply hold a basketball in your upturned hand—like a waiter would hold a tray—and release your wrist forward so the ball rolls off the tips of your fingers. As you begin the shooting motion, one of the main variables for how far the ball travels is how quickly you release your wrist. The ball will always go straight on target if your elbow and wrist release stay in line without any twist to your forearm.

The exact same physics are at work on your putting stroke. If you take your stance, and set your grip in the lifeline of your right hand so that it aligns with your forearm, your right wrist will work the same way as your wrist works when you're shooting a basketball, bending right in line with the forearm. On the backswing, you load your right wrist by bending it back, then unload the wrist through the ball. The more aggressively you unload the wrist, the more energy you produce in the swing. Producing this energy makes it much easier to use the weight of the club to get the putter swinging on plane every time. When you begin to swing the putterhead freely and on plane, you'll make solid contact and your speed control will come naturally. Remember, the goal here is to swing in a good sequence. Even though this swing thought might make you feel "wristy," the stroke won't *look* wristy. It'll look great.

The actual movement of the putter and your body on a 10- or 15-foot putt is pretty small. You're looking for a single feel or swing thought that allows the putterhead to move in sequence on the backswing and flow down through the ball in a natural, repeatable way. To me, the best way to do that is to look for

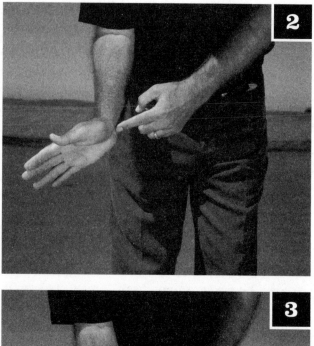

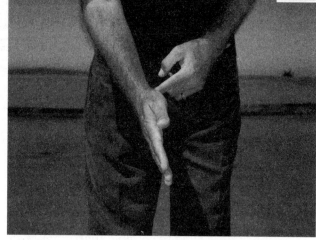

SNAP IT!

When you shoot a basketball (as a right-hander), your right forearm is vertical (1) and the power for the shot comes from the wrist extending straight from the arm. This wrist movement is the same in a putt, just angled toward the ball. On the backswing, the wrist hinges in line with the forearm (2), then straightens on the downswing (3) back to the point where the top of the wrist, hand and arm are flat.

feels that promote the head swinging. That's getting gravity and physics to work for you, not against you.

I'm always looking for specific feels that encourage the grip to move very little while the head swings. I've had success concentrating on releasing tension in my shoulders before my practice swing. Tension in the shoulder and elbow joints as well as in the forearms encourages you to move your entire upper body as a unit. Another good swing thought is the feeling of softness in the right elbow on the takeaway. When the right wrist hinges in the basketball move I just described, a soft right elbow absorbs that movement and promotes the swinging of the clubhead.

Conversely, another great feel is that of the right elbow extending on the downswing and the left elbow softening. Moving the focus from what the hands are doing to what the elbows are doing seems to release a lot of tension and prevent the manipulation of the club for many players. A related downswing thought is the feel of the right forearm rotating toward the target through impact. That rotation pushes the speed down to the clubhead end—a much better technique than keeping the forearm rigid and shoving the grip toward the target on the downswing, which usually results in an open face and pushed putts.

Practicing one-handed putts with only the right hand is another way to isolate some of these feels for use later, when you've got both hands on the putter. Let the wrist bend and load on the backswing—it will have to for you to be able to generate any kind of swing—and for the right elbow to soften and move along your side. Then let the right elbow extend and the forearm to rotate through impact so that the putter continues along an arcing path to the finish.

One feel-related subject I'm asked about a lot are the yips. What are they, and how do you fix them? I'm not a psychologist, so I can't speak about some of the theories other instructors have, which basically say that the yips are in your head. My experience with students has been that most of those who come to me with what they call a yips issue—either in putting or chipping—have mechanical issues that seem to be the underlying cause of the flinch. With bad ball position or mechanics that promote the club coming through impact without being square, the brain subconsciously knows something drastic has to happen to get the ball back on target, so it fires muscles to twist the face back into position. Once the player starts feeling that flinch, it's understandable that he would freak out and start tinkering with his setup and stroke.

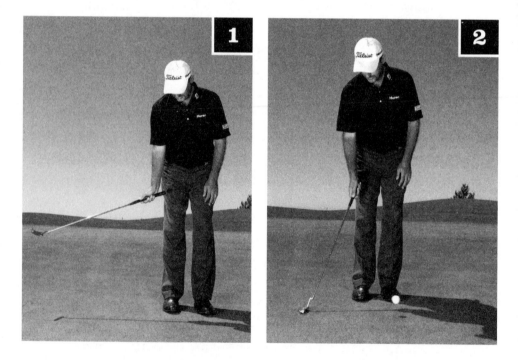

**To smooth a yip-influenced stroke, move the ball two feet back in your stance and start by holding the club near waist high with just the right hand (1). Hit the ball by simply dropping the club down, letting the wrist unhinge from the weight of the clubhead, not through any effort (2).**

To clean all of that out, I start players off with a simple one-handed drill. Moving the ball dramatically back in the stance, I ask them to simply hold the putter in one hand, lift it and drop the head down on the ball, letting gravity do all the work. I want them to feel how substantial the weight of the putterhead really is, and how just letting it fall can get the job done. I'm not taking wrist action away from the player with the yips, I'm showing him how to use the wrists correctly. A session simply walking around the green and dropping the putter on the ball like this does wonders for smoothing out the stroke—assuming the player also gets himself back into the neutral setup fundamentals we talked about in Chapter 1.

## SWING FEELS

The full swing obviously has more moving parts—which makes having a simple swing thought or feel both harder *and* more important. It's easy to get swamped with mechanical thoughts when you're on the range or out on the golf course. Head down, full turn, shift the weight, release club, full finish, balance. There are dozens of feel "code words" in golf.

Picking the right feel to go with at a given time is a two-pronged process. First, you have to uncover what swing thoughts or feels are actually productive for you. Which ones work? Second, it's not necessarily as simple as picking something from a list of perfect form elements or swing mechanics. As we've been talking about for half a book now, holding the club the right way or having it in a certain position at a certain time doesn't mean the swing holds together as a coherent whole.

The goal is to choose a swing thought or feel that gets your body (and the club) to do what you want it to do. Sometimes the feel or thought runs counter to physics—and to what you actually *do*. For example, I've heard a teacher give a student a lesson and tell him to swing the driver back without letting the clubhead get behind him. That's almost physically impossible to do, of course. But the thought of it—the feel that the teacher gave him—caused the player to stop pulling the clubhead to the inside on the takeaway. The player's feel wasn't technically "accurate," but it got him doing what he should be doing.

How do you find a feel that works? Try a lot of them. Try to determine if you're a player who responds more to watching somebody else and copying, or to hearing a description, or to having a teacher actually put his or her hands on you to make a certain move. However you respond best, pick that train of thought and hit balls and play practice rounds while incorporating a single feel or swing thought into your pre-shot routine. All of the various swing mechanics and form elements we've been talking about are important, but your brain just can't synthesize all those thoughts at once a millisecond before you start your swing. Picking one—one that has the most positive impact on your sequencing that day—is the most profitable move.

Just like in putting, I find that the best full-swing thoughts (and short-game thoughts, for that matter) are the ones that connect me with the speed of the clubhead. I want to connect my feel to my effort to make the clubhead go faster. Unless I'm dealing with a specific cause-and-effect situation—like concentrating on my hips turning when I'm under pressure—I'm thinking about a hands-related feel in my pre-shot routine. I've found that to be productive for most of the players I teach.

If you're a visual person, it can really be helpful to think of an exaggerated situation that produces the effect you're looking for in your swing. In a golf swing, your wrists should release the club right down the plane line (more on that in the next chapter) like a hammer pounding a nail. If I handed you an actual hammer, you wouldn't even think about technique. You'd just

On a good swing, a golf club unhinges through impact the same way a hammer does when striking a nail. In this case, the hammer strike comes from a bent over golf posture (1) and the nail is angled into the ground on the same plane as the swing. If you drop your right shoulder to try to lift the ball (2), the hammer will swing over the nail. Roll your forearms in an effort to release the club and the face of the hammer will miss the target (3).

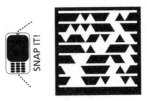

SNAP IT!

pound the nail, and you'd use a wrist hinge that's perfect for the golf swing. Now imagine holding a hammer in front of you in your golf posture, with both hands. If a club shaft is sticking in the ground at the plane angle of your swing, your motion should produce a release of the hammer right down onto the shaft, pounding it into the ground. If you tilt your shoulders to try to lift the ball, you'll swing the hammer right over the top of the shaft. If you roll your forearms instead of hinging your wrists, you'll roll the face of the hammer right over the shaft instead of pounding it in, and you'll hit it with the flat side. The hammer image is a great full-swing feel, and I use it with a lot of students.

On short-game shots, my feels or swing thoughts are usually connected to making the clubhead release sooner or later in the downswing. The time of the release determines how much loft the shot has (as we've discussed), and how much of the bounce on the bottom of the club is exposed. On high-lofted shots or bunker explosions, trying to feel as though you're skipping a rock across the water is a great swing thought. This feel really promotes the underhanded early release you need to get the bounce of the club skipping through the sand. On a low, running shot, my feel is just the opposite. I want my body turn to lead the downswing, while the clubhead and my hands trail behind. On those shots, a great feel is one in which you imagine that there's a rope around the clubhead, and that somebody behind you is giving the rope a tug just as you start your downswing. That instant of resistance on the head starts a great downswing sequence that almost can't help but produce solid shots.

# Chapter 6

# ONE CLUB, FIVE SHOTS

. . . . . . . . . . . . . . . . . . . . . . . . . . . . . . . . . . . . . . . . . . . . .

U nderstanding the basic mechanics that go into the different shots you hit—and how the concept of sequencing applies to those shots—is what I would call "school." You have to learn the basics and repeat the lessons, and the tests come at the end, when it's time to go out into the real world.

Now that we've spent some time talking about the form, the sequence and the feel of different shots, I want to take those lessons out of the classroom and onto the course to show how they fit together within your entire golf game.

And I'm going to do it with one club—my 58-degree wedge.

Why one club? It's simple—literally and figuratively. When I do a large clinic, some of the first questions I always get are about club selection for different shots around the green. People want to know if they should use a 7-iron for a bump-and-run shot, or if buying a 64-degree wedge like the one Phil Mickelson popularized would help them hit high, soft-landing pitch shots. I answer yes. Yes—a low-lofted club or a super-high lofted club would work on those kinds of shots. But I believe doing it that way isn't always the simplest way.

I believe the easiest way to hit consistently good shots and develop better touch and feel is to take one club and make it your short-game specialty club. Then take the time to learn the ins and outs of that one club—what you need to do to make shots go high or low, long or short. By getting way more practice time and reps with one club, you're going to be more comfortable and confident with it. You won't have to guess how far your 7-iron will hit a bump-and-run shot, or try to remember the last time you hit that same kind of shot two or three rounds ago. And you won't need to carry a 64-degree wedge in your bag for the one or two times you might need to hit it over eighteen holes.

Understanding how to play different shots with the same go-to club will make you a complete player. You'll also have a better chance of manufacturing a specialty shot for a unique situation using a club you've hit with a million times before. I'm not saying it's wrong to use different clubs around the green. In fact, I believe it's a good idea to putt or use a hybrid from off the green if you aren't feeling comfortable with your short game or you have a bare lie. But I believe you'll get the most consistent positive results from learning the vagaries of one wedge and building a collection of different shots with that wedge.

We've talked about some of the setup and sequencing basics for the shots I'm going to describe here, but in this chapter, I want to explain the context of each shot—when you use it and how to hit it most effectively for the given circumstance. And you can hit every one of these with the same club—a 58-degree wedge with 10 degrees of bounce. It's the club I use for 95 percent of my short-game shots. By modifying your body position at address, changing the angle of the shaft or the face at address, or changing the sequence or the speed at which you release the clubhead through impact, you can make the same club hit an endless list of shots. I'll describe five of them here.

Let's talk about the low chip-and-run, lofted pitch, bunker shot, trouble shot, and distance pitch—five shots that together cover virtually any situation you might encounter out on the course.

# LOW CHIP-AND-RUN

I define a chip-and-run or bump-and-run shot as a shot that rolls more than it flies—usually to a target with a lot of available green around it. If you're just off the green in fairway grass, and the flag is 20 yards on and not protected by a tier or other obstacle, running a low shot up to the hole like a putt is often the best play. Basically, the loft on the wedge is going to shoot the ball low into the air to carry the fairway cut of grass and land just onto the surface of the green.

For a low-running shot, you're hitting the ball first, then bottoming out the swing just in front of the ball. The key to doing that successfully is to preset your spine tilt left and your weight on your forward foot at address, then keep it there throughout the shot. Then you pivot around your left leg, with the grip of the club moving very little. You're simply hinging the wrists and making a slight hip turn on the backswing, then letting the clubhead fall back to the ground as you make a hip turn through impact.

How much weight should you have forward? I feel as though 65 or 70 percent of my weight is on my left foot. But I bet that if we had access to a foot-pressure-distribution monitor—yes, they have those now—that measured it precisely, and I blind-folded you and adjusted your weight until you got 70 percent of it on your lead foot, you'd swear that 90 percent of your weight was forward. That's because so many players are used to setting up with neutral weight distribution, or even with their weight shifted back, because it feels "natural" to tilt your spine away from the target so you can add loft to the clubface to get the ball in the air. You've probably also heard a million times—and in a million instruction articles—that you need to open your stance and move the ball back to chip. But that combination of factors—the ball back, the right spine tilt and the weight shift away from the target because of the open stance—leads to less solid impact, because you have to play the shot with an open face and a swing path that goes to the left.

The easiest way to set yourself with a good forward spine tilt is to have your right shoulder a little higher than the left at setup. You may also want to try and have your right hip higher than the left. Now your spine tilt is forward, but your hips are close to level, and you have the perfect combination. When you make your swing, feel yourself keeping your hips and shoulders level all the way through. If you let your right shoulder dip, you're moving the bottom of the swing back, behind the ball. By staying level, the club moves around your body on plane and compresses the ball, the key to crisp contact.

Many players also mess this shot up by making a huge arm swing on the backswing, which often leads to drastically reduced wrist action. They swing the arms down fast for most of the way, but then the brain reminds them that the shot only needs to go 40 feet, so the arms slow way down. The body stays tilted away from the target, and the swing bottoms out behind the ball. From there, the only thing you can do is scoop the hands at the ball and get lucky. But mostly, you'll hit it thin or fat.

By combining a pivot with a small arm swing and letting gravity drop the clubhead onto the ball, you're controlling the length of the shot with the size and speed of your pivot. For a 10-yard chip, the hips might turn only a few degrees. For a 40-yard chip, the turn might be two-thirds as full as one you'd use on a full shot. Letting the pivot control the distance also helps you fight the urge to fire your right hand in an attempt to lift the ball.

As we discussed in Chapter 3, the left hand controls the clubface during this motion. The more you turn your left hand down toward the ball through impact, the lower the shot will fly. I like to have my students practice until they have a sense for how far the ball will fly versus roll as they gain control over this combination of turning down the face and pivoting technique. They will usually settle on the feel they can control and then begin to see the shot they want to play from different situations.

I don't have a technical, cut-and-dried system for how far the ball should fly and how far it should roll out when playing my shots around the green. I believe that every situation calls for reading your lie and the firmness of the green and using the shot that you feel most comfortable with and that best suits what you need to do. That being said, when there's room to do so, I tend to play shots that roll out a greater distance than they fly in the air. Once you gain some confidence, you'll want to make sure that you're reading the portion of the chip that is rolling along the ground just as you would if you were putting. I'm trying to hole my bump-and-run chips just as I am my putts. Once you've mastered the relatively simple move, it's a higher-percentage play than putting from the fringe, because the wedge gets the ball up and over the higher cut of grass— where it could get knocked slightly off line if you tried to putt. When you watch PGA Tour events, you'll see players hit this shot with the pin pulled out, because they're actually more confident of holing one from 20 or 30 feet with this technique than they would be on a putt of the same length. That should tell you something.

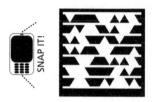

# LOFTED PITCH

I define a lofted pitch as a high-flying shot that is hit by releasing the clubhead and using the bounce on the bottom of the club. It goes high and lands softly, coming to a stop more because of the loft on the shot than any backspin put on the ball. When hitting the chip-and-run, I've got the shaft of the club angled slightly forward at address, with the handle a little closer to the target than the head. On a lofted pitch, the club should be vertical, which gives the face more loft. Notice I didn't say that I open the clubface. I think the face should be relatively square, along with your stance, because you want to be able to take true aim at the target instead of trying to calculate how the open face and open stance will affect where the ball goes.

In order to simplify this shot, I change my setup a little. I move a little farther away from the ball—two or three inches—which causes me to bend over a little more and sets my hands lower. This changes the swing plane slightly. By shallowing the angle of attack on the ball—making it move more around my body, rather than up and down—it makes it easier to hit a softer shot and allows a little more room for error, because the clubhead travels closer to the ground for slightly longer. It's important to remember to back up from the ball to get your hands lower—you don't want to just lower them from your original stance. This bit of extra room will make it easier to fully release the clubhead at impact, which returns the face back to neutral loft.

On both the chip-and-run and lofted pitch, I play the ball from the middle of my stance, with my weight and spine tilt slightly forward. My stance is slightly wider on the lofted pitch—five or six inches between my heels instead of two or three—in order to make it easier to lower my hands and shallow out my swing.

Once I've made these subtle setup changes, the big difference in hitting the shot comes from the sequencing of the release. On the chip-and-run, I'm not doing any conscious firing of my right hand, just turning the clubface down through impact. On a lofted pitch, I want to use the bounce on the bottom of the club to skim the turf under the ball, and I want the loft on the club to increase through impact. I do that by releasing the club earlier in the downswing—in a way that feels like a sidearm or underhand move with my right hand. After impact, it should feel as though your right palm is facing up—like you've just skipped a rock across the water.

To achieve this free release of the clubhead down through impact, it helps to have a neutral grip—the same one we talked about for full-swing shots. If your grip is too strong (or turned much too far to the right, especially in your right hand) you'll struggle to get the clubhead to release the way that I've described. If it's too weak (turned too far to the left), you'll tend to come through with the clubface very open, or over-rotate on the release and dig the leading edge of the club into the turf. To check your grip to see if it is strong, weak, or neutral, set your hands on the club and hold it in front of you about waist high. Now raise and lower it with your wrists, straight up and down. The leading edge of the clubhead will remain vertical if you have your hands in the neutral position. If the toe of the club leans left, your grip is too strong. If it leans to the right, your grip is too weak.

When you get the bottom of the club skipping along the ground, you've given yourself a tremendous weapon, because you have a good three-inch-long area at the bottom of the swing where you can contact the ball and still produce a decent shot. Hit two inches behind the ball, like a bunker shot, and you'll hit a high floater without too much spin. Catch the ball more cleanly and it will go farther, but with more backspin and check.

Adding the lofted pitch to your repertoire of shots is important because you obviously don't always have enough green around the hole to roll the ball up. I use a lofted pitch to carry a shot over heavily contoured areas on the green and to get the ball up on the same tier as the flag. For example, if you have 20 yards between the ball and the hole—three yards of fringe, 12 yards of contoured green and a tier, and then five yards from the top of the tier to the hole, it would be a complicated piece of trigonometry to determine the best way to roll the ball through the breaks and up the tier to settle by the hole. The lofted pitch allows you to fly the ball up to the tier and drop it softly beside the hole.

Controlling distance on a lofted pitch is similar to the technique you'd use on the chip-and-run. You pivot back and through, and the size and speed of the pivot is the main accelerator pedal for the shot. The one difference is that the release of the clubhead is another speed generator. One way to think about it is that the body turn and pivot provide the distance for the shot, while the release and hand speed provide the height. The main thing you need to differentiate, though, is hand speed versus arm speed. The release we're talking about here is the uncocking of the wrists. Speed comes from the clubhead moving faster—not from the arms moving faster. An extremely common mistake is swinging the arms fast from the top of the backswing—which can actually slow down the clubhead because the grip end speeds up and leaves the clubhead behind, rather than speeding it up like you want it to. Feel that same level turn back and through as you did for the chip-and-run, and get the sense that your arms are staying close to your body during the entire downswing. After impact, the hands stay low and move around your body to the left pocket of your pants at the finish.

You can lock down the fundamentals and sequencing for this shot, but that work will get lost if you don't get more precise—and careful—when picking your target. One of the most common strategy mistakes I see comes from players who focus on the flag—rather than the landing point—as their target. It's understandable—after all, the hole is the ultimate goal. But when you've determined that a lofted pitch is the shot that fits your situation, you must take care to step off the yardage to your ideal landing spot, and then go through your pre-shot and aiming routines with your focus on that landing spot, not on the hole. How big of a spot are we talking about? That depends on your skill level. I pick a spot that's smaller than the size of a basketball hoop. You might pick a hula hoop–sized target. Whatever size you pick is fine, as long as you have a defined target that you can lock into and that's easy to see, so you can tell if you hit your target or not. You need to be able to measure yourself against your plan so you can come away from the round with an idea of which part of your game needs the work.

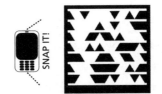

# BUNKER SHOT AND TROUBLE SHOT

We're going to talk about the bunker shot and trouble shot together—and right after the high pitch—because they're similar to each other and fundamentally similar to the high pitch. The goal for all three shots is the same: Get the bounce on the bottom of the club exposed to the ground and the clubface in position to pop the ball in the air and out of sand or deep grass.

We've talked about the importance of forward spine tilt on the chip-and-run and lofted pitch, and it's an even bigger deal here, when you're trying to make contact in a consistent spot and produce height. If you set up for a greenside bunker shot the "conventional" way, with a wide open stance and the ball forward, you're presetting your right shoulder dramatically lower than your left, and this shoulder tilt encourages you to shallow out your swing with your body instead of the release of the club—which causes the clubhead to crash into the sand way too far behind the ball. I want to use my left spine tilt to create a steeper angle on my swing, and at the same time release the clubhead early with my hands back to create the skipping action and added loft on the clubface to hit a very soft shot. The other added bonus and possibly the most important one regarding maintaining the left spine tilt is that I can trust the bottom of my swing to stay at home or in the same place all the time. This one fundamental will help you eliminate the fear of skulling your pitch shots or catching them fat.

The technique I teach came from a lesson I got from Tom Pernice many years ago. It looks kind of strange, but after you try it a few times you'll understand why I think it's so easy that it's almost like cheating. The setup is somewhat similar to that of the lofted pitch—a vertical or slightly backward-leaning shaft, and hands set lower because I'm standing a few inches farther from the ball at address—but with a much wider stance.

I set up with my feet wider than they would be for even a driver, with the same forward spine tilt that we've been talking about. Ball position is only a little in front of the middle of your stance. I do open the clubface slightly on these shots to get more of the bounce exposed to the sand. By lowering my hands, I've created a much flatter shaft angle, and steeper swing plane. An extra bonus is that when you lower your hands this way, it effectively neutralizes the slightly open clubface in terms of your aim. You can still confidently go right at your target.

When you swing, you're essentially going to pick the clubhead up with your wrists as you make your hip and shoulder turn, then throw it down at the sand early in your downswing. You maintain your weight on your front foot, and with that wide stance it will feel like a reverse pivot when you swing—but if you feel that, you're doing it right. At impact, you want to stop the grip end of the club and try to make the clubhead whip through as though you were snapping a towel, then finish with the shaft straight up and down. The only way to get the shaft vertical like that is to stop the grip end. If you push the grip through impact and down the target line, you'll dig the leading edge into the sand and either hit it fat or blade it.

If you maintain your same spine tilt from address all the way through the swing, you'll be able to contact the sand (or the grass, in the case of a trouble shot) in a very precise place. Since there's no weight shift, the bottom of your swing is going to be in line with the tip of your nose. That's especially helpful when dealing with different sand and grass conditions, where it might make sense to hit closer to or farther away from the ball.

The beauty of this bunker technique is that it works perfectly on *any* shot where you don't have a good lie and you need to hit something high and soft. You can use it from deep grass around the green, a divot, or even a wet, muddy lie. Set up exactly as you would for a bunker shot, and control the height

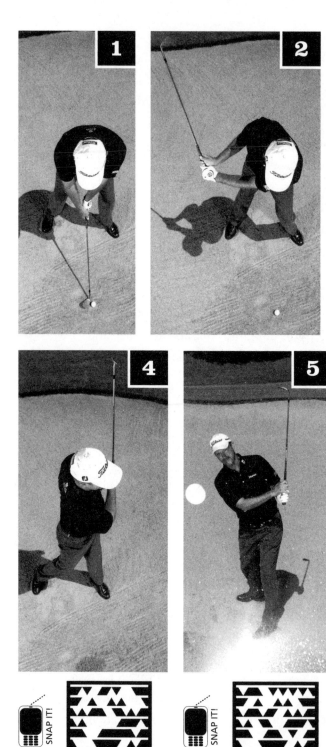

My bunker setup features a wide stance—wider than for a driver—and level shoulders (1). Notice how my shoulders have turned, but my head is in the same place it was at address (2), indicating no weight shift. I throw the clubhead through impact so that it passes the grip end before it gets to the ball, which keeps the bounce exposed to the sand (3). My hands move around my body and stay low, and my shoulders are still level, as they were throughout the swing (4). By stopping the grip, the club returns to vertical very soon after impact (5).

SNAP IT!

SNAP IT!

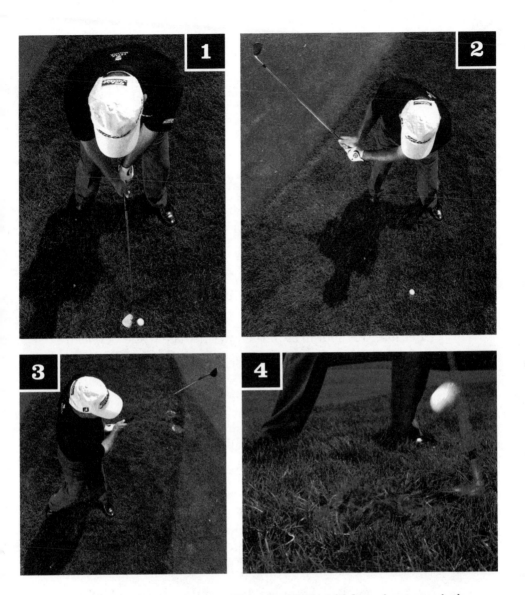

SNAP IT!

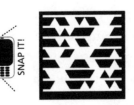

The setup for a trouble shot (1) from deep grass is the same as for a bunker shot, with a wide stance and the shaft leaning backward, away from the target. On the backswing, my right elbow slides along my side as I aggressively hinge my wrists (2). My weight stays planted on my front foot. Through the finish, my hands stay low and move around to my left front pocket (3) as I keep the bounce of the club pointed at the ground. As the clubhead goes through the grass, the leading edge cuts through the grass while the bounce skips along the ground below (4).

and distance of the shot with the speed of your release and the size of the swing. The faster you release the clubhead and the closer you hit to the ball, the more backspin you'll produce.

# DISTANCE PITCH

A distance pitch is an interesting shot in that it's the last step between a short-game shot and a full swing. Many, many players—including tour players I've worked with over the years—dislike the 50- or 60-yard pitch shot more than any other. They struggle with making a less than full swing for a shot that is far enough from the green that they don't feel like they have a dialed-in sense of touch.

Because this shot lives in the intermediate world between a short-game swing and a full swing, players feel like they have to dial down the speed. The problems crop up when they dial down the speed the wrong way. The most common mistake I see is that players essentially freeze the lower body and turn this into an all-arms shot. When all you're doing is waving your arms at the ball, at best you'll have a hard time with distance control.

To get a feel for how the lower body should pivot on a distance pitch, and how the arms should work in conjunction with that fluid, athletic lower-body motion (instead of leading in an awkward yank down from the top of the backswing) try this drill with a golf ball. Set up in your regular stance and hold the ball in your right hand. Now pivot and throw the ball underhand as far as you can down the range. If you freeze your lower body and just sling it with your arm, it's almost impossible to throw the ball more than 20 feet. But if you make a pivot and let your arm follow your body turn, you amplify the slinging motion dramatically, and you can make a long toss.

Another aspect of good distance pitching is revealed through the underhand toss drill. If you squeeze the ball really hard and try to toss the ball with flexed, tight muscles in your arms and legs, you can't throw the ball very far, or with any touch. But if you feel the weight of the ball in your hand and let your body respond to that weight with loose muscles, you not only get more speed on the throw, you have more touch when it comes to how far you choose to throw it. If somebody told you to toss the ball underhanded into a wastebasket 10 feet away, you wouldn't tense your entire body and try to balance the ball on your outstretched hand and shove it toward the basket. You'd flex your knees and your arm and hold the ball in your fingertips to get some feel into the throw. The same is true for a golf shot.

Much like the chip-and-run and lofted pitch, the size and speed of your pivot is the main driver for determining the distance you hit this shot. The more you turn back with your hips and shoulders in the backswing and the faster you rotate through in the downswing, the longer the shot will fly.

The last element in controlling distance on an intermediate pitch shot is changing trajectory. As I said before, I prefer to hit these shots as low as I can get away with. I believe that I can control the distance that I need the ball to fly more easily with a low trajectory than with a high one. When I'm playing the low shot and using my pivot correctly, I can count on pinching the ball at impact and having it take a couple of hops and checks, then releases up to the hole. I think almost every tour player would say he or she prefers to hit this type of shot to the green versus the really high, middle-range wedge shot.

In order to play this lower-trajectory shot, I keep my weight mostly forward as I make my backswing turn. I bow my left wrist down slightly in the takeaway as well to reduce loft off the clubface. I always try to keep my arm swing to a minimum.

When I make my pivot to start the downswing, the body turn pulls my arms around my body, with the clubhead moving around and out in front of me onto the plane. Because I've started my pivot by getting my left leg straightened and out of the way, I have room to turn my right side through to the finish level and on top of the ball. This is what it means when you hear a teacher say that you need to "cover the ball." You're moving your body in a way that makes the clubhead come around and trap the ball against the ground. The reduced loft and square hit compresses the ball and produces a penetrating, accurate ball flight—something you don't get if you cut across the ball or hit it with an open clubface. By playing the shot this way, you'll quickly develop a sense for the connection between the size of the swing and the distance the ball flies. You won't have to make any adjustments because you're hitting the ball with a glancing blow, or because you're aiming to the left in an open stance.

One thing that many first-time students are surprised about is that I don't want this shot to rely on backspin. In fact, I teach tour players like Sergio Garcia how to hit it with less hand action so that they can *reduce* backspin. Average players watch a lot of television golf and see players jamming shots right up by the hole and stopping the ball with dramatic backspin—even with the new rules on groove depth in wedges. There might be an occasional need for that kind of shot, but it's a challenge to make that kind of perfect contact every time—even for a tour player. What you don't see is that the guy who is slightly off his game leaves these important scoring wedge shots 15 or 20 feet away. (You don't see it because he missed the cut and is on his way home.) Playing a more neutral, safe roll-out shot is much more consistent and gives you more good chances to get up and down—without the theatrics.

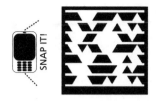

SNAP IT!

As I said earlier in this chapter, I hit all of these shots with a 58-degree wedge with 10 degrees of bounce. I like that combination of loft and bounce because it's flexible enough to use out of the bunker, from the fairway, and from a tight, firm lie. I have the bounce on my Titleist Vokey sand wedge modified to be even more flexible. The bounce material near the toe and near the heel has been ground away, so if I play a shot with the club more upright or the face more open, the club still rests flat on the ground, but I keep the benefit of the bounce under the middle of the face for more standard shots. I have my wedges customized just for me by the guys in the Titleist tour van, but you can get something similar delivered right to your door. Titleist now sells Vokey wedges with six different specialized tour grinds with varying degrees of bounce wrap and camber. My wedge is closest to the "M" grind—the model that's probably the best pick for those who play in a variety of course conditions.

Could you go through this menu of shots and play them all with your 56-degree or 60-degree club? Absolutely. You might give up some flexibility or ease of execution on one end or another with clubs of those lofts, but I believe you're going to have a better overall game if you start with the one short-game club you feel the most comfortable with. When you find that club, use it as the basis to build the other wedges in your set.

Here you can see the relationship between the backswings of a pitch shot (**1**) and full wedge (**2**): The full wedge shot has more hip and shoulder turn, and the wrists have cocked to produce more clubhead speed. Although there are many opinions about what moves first in the downswing, remember one thing: The clubhead has the longest distance to travel.

When I talk about swinging the putter on-plane, I'm referring to the putter moving on a slight curve, as shown here using the Learning Curve teaching aid. The path of the stroke is a curve, but the second component of it is equally important: The face of the putter has to remain square to the path. Notice the hash lines extending perpendicular from the arc at each point in the swing. Those hashes indicate a square position relative to the path of the putter. If you swing the putter on the arc but rotate the face open or hold it shut on the backswing, you have to manipulate it through impact to send the ball on target.

• • • • • • • • • • • • • • •

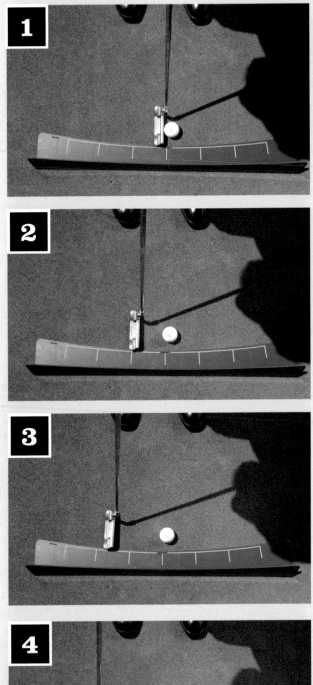

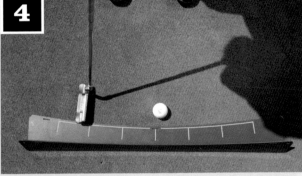

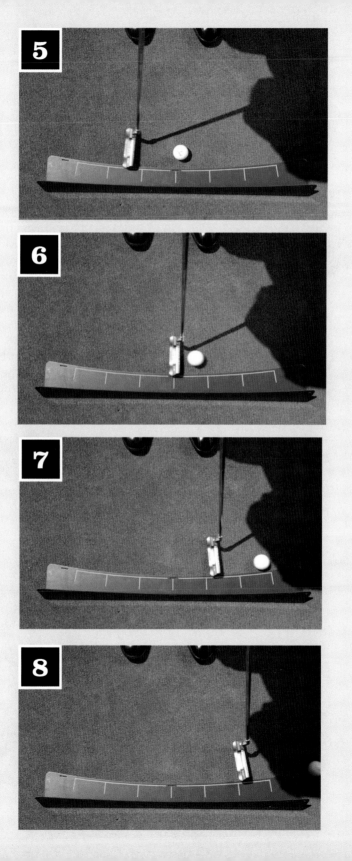

**1**

From this overhead view of a standard bunker shot, you can really see how much the different pieces of the swing—the body, the grip, and the clubhead—move in relation to each other. The curved training aid at my feet (**1**) shows the path my hands take during the swing. At the start of the backswing, my body hasn't moved much at all (**2**), while my hands have traced the curve and the clubhead has moved the most. At the top of the backswing (**3**), my body has made a turn, and my hands have reached the end of the curve on the ground, while the clubhead has moved even more with the hinge in my wrists. On the downswing, my hands follow the curve around and finish near my left pocket (**4**), and the shaft of the club moves into a vertical position.

**2**

**1**

On any shot, the shoulders should move on a relatively level plane (**1**). Resist the tendency to lower your back shoulder (**2**) to try to help the ball in the air. In the third photo (**3**), I'm hitting an extremely lofted pitch, but my shoulders are still turning relatively level. I'm using the release of the clubhead to provide the loft and speed. On a full iron shot (**4**) the clubhead lags slightly behind the hands and grip through impact, compressing the ball.

• • • • • • • • • • • • • • • • • • • •

**2**

When you look from overhead at a trouble shot from high rough, you can see how similar it is to a bunker shot. In fact, it's identical. The setup is the same (1), with a square stance, shaft leaning slightly away from the target and clubhead slightly open. I make a narrow backswing (2), with my right elbow moving back along my side, then throw the clubhead at a spot behind the ball and finish near my left pocket (3), just like the bunker shot.

# Chapter 7

# THE FULL SWING

. . . . . . . . . . . . . . . . . . . . . . . . . . . . . . . . . . . . . . . . . . . . . .

One of the most interesting by-products of the short-game teaching I've been doing with dedicated amateur players over the past six or seven years has been the feedback they've given me about their full swings. More and more, I hear from them that what I've been saying about the short game—the sequencing of the body and club and the releasing of the clubhead—not only matches what they're hearing from their full-swing teacher, but improves their full swing as a part of the deal.

Hearing those comments—and spending many hours talking to teacher friends Jim Hardy and Mike Adams—helped me to better understand the connection between short-game sequencing and the full swing, and built my confidence in helping average players get better with their whole game.

As you move from a 10-foot putt to a chip shot to an intermediate pitch to a full swing, you're playing the same game and essentially making the same motion, but with more movement on the clubhead end and added turn and pivot. So it stands to reason that you can use the mechanics and sequencing basics you've learned on shorter shots to "grow" into your full swing.

Let's examine that idea.

On that 10-foot putt, the clubhead moves about 15 inches in each direction. As we discussed in the first two chapters, the head moves the most, while each subsequent piece of the puzzle—the hands, arms, and body—moves progressively less. That's the basic description of the sequencing of a putting stroke. When you hit a pitch shot, the swing itself gets larger, because the clubhead has to move farther—four or five feet. As the clubhead travels a longer distance, the arms swing slightly more and the body responds with more of a turn back and more of a pivot through. You're adding pieces to the swing in order.

The golf swing moves in a circle, whether we're talking about a putt or a tee shot. The putt swing traces a small slice of the circle, while the tee shot traces an almost 360-degree path, but both are on a tilted circle. My goal for you is to understand how each shot relates to that circle, and how to sequence the club to keep it moving on that circle in the most efficient way.

I'm going to refer to that circle as the "plane," but I need to give some background here so that you don't get confused with some other ways the term "plane" has been used in golf instruction. My friend Jim Hardy has revolutionized the way teachers look at the full swing by creating a kind of sorting system for the way players' bodies, arms, and club move. He uses the terms "one-plane" and "two-plane" to describe how the angle or direction the left arm moves during the swing compared with the angle that the shoulders turn on during the swing. If a player swings more around his body and the plane of his left arm and shoulders match when viewed from down the target line (where you'd stand if you were watching a player from behind on the range), he's a "one-plane" swinger. This is most common in players who have a fair amount of spine tilt toward the ball either at setup or especially at impact, because they bend down closer to the ball on the downswing. Ben Hogan, Sam Snead, and Tiger Woods (with his irons) are famous one-plane swingers. If a player lifts the club with his arms onto a steeper plane while his shoulders and body turn fairly level during the swing, he's a "two-plane" swinger. These players usually have rather upright setup positions. Jack Nicklaus, Tom Watson and Payne Stewart are famous two-plane swingers.

Jim's plane concepts are terrific and valid—I work on my own full swing with him, and I'm becoming a much better ball-striker as a one-planer (which, by the way, was the swing I always used for my wedge shots). But I'm going to leave that particular kind of plane discussion for more in-depth full-swing books. When I talk about the concept of "plane" here in this chapter, I'm referring to the plane the club itself swings on—as determined by the club's shaft. Whatever planes your arms and body swing on, the goal of swinging the club in a consistent circle—the plane on which the shaft swings around your body so that the clubhead can make contact with the ground—is the same.

The fundamentals of the game of golf have been the same forever. My simple way of looking at it is that no matter what club or ball has been used throughout the centuries, the ball is on the ground and the player stands off to the side. Other than having both hands on the club, it isn't much different than swinging a stick at a rock on the ground. The ball is out to the side of us, and I like to use one of Mr. Hardy's phrases: "Golf is a side-on game." If you look at the way that the club is built, it has a shaft and a head for hitting the ball that's set at an angle to the shaft. Although there are many different ways to swing the club and play good golf—just look at Miller Barber, Lee Trevino, or Jim Furyk—the fact remains that the players who make golf look effortless are the ones whose club shafts swing in a smooth and uninterrupted circle. (Steve Elkington and Mark O'Meara come to mind when I think of players who always make hitting the ball look easy.) If the club swings on in a circle and remains pointed back toward or near the ball throughout the swing, the game will be easier than if the club wanders off track and has to be rerouted, no matter what shot you're playing—from putt to full swing. If you stood to the side of the ball and swung the club on a too-upright swing plane, you'd miss the ball to the inside, closer to your feet, and crash the club into the ground. If you stood to the side and swung on a plane that was too flat, you'd miss the ball and the ground completely—a completely flat swing plane, in fact, would be similar to a baseball swing. Jim Hardy equates swing plane to landing an airplane. If the airplane has too steep an angle of attack, it will crash into the ground. If the angle is too flat, the plane will never touch down. The ideal plane has the right mix of up and down and around.

How do you determine the right swing plane for you? It depends somewhat on your height and the club you're using. But I want you to find your swing plane by using speed to determine where your body and arms naturally want to go. Make some swings while holding the club up around belt high, as you would a baseball bat. Make sure you're turning your hips and shoulders back and through as well as flinging the club around your body as fast as possible with your wrists and arms. Sense the releasing of your wrists and the rolling over of your forearms. Continue swinging back and forth without stopping. Once you think you're reaching full speed, simply bend over and brush the ground. You've just established your natural swing plane. It's that simple. The faster you move the club, the more true the circle will remain as you swing the club around your body. It's when you try to muscle the grip and put the club into a certain position that the circle gets knocked out of round and the game gets harder.

The second element to the swing plane is the club you're using for a given shot. Because a short iron is built with a shorter shaft and a more upright lie angle, you're going to have a more upright swing plane with that club than you would with your driver, which has a longer shaft and a flatter lie angle. That fits into what you probably already understand about a driver swing—it's a more around-the-body, sweeping motion—versus a putt or a short-iron swing.

The tilt of the swing plane—the angle at which it sits in relation to the ball—is one piece of the puzzle. The direction of the swing plane is the second critical element. Imagine a hula hoop resting flat on the ground. If you walked over and got in your golf stance and then lifted the side of the hoop closest to you until it was at a 45-degree angle to the ground, you would have established the tilt of the hoop. Holding the edge of the hoop closest to you, if you then twist the hoop as though you were going to roll it to the right or left, you've changed the direction of the swing plane.

Your goal in a golf swing is to move the club on a consistent swing plane so that the clubhead hits the ball in the direction you choose. Setting up and sequencing your swing in a way that does that makes the game way easier.

The same things that interrupt a good swing plane on a putt or a chip shot cause the problems in a full swing. It starts with setup and aim. One of the baseline checks I make during a putting lesson is to have the player set up so that his feet, hips, and shoulders are all aimed the same way—parallel to the target line. Many players who struggle with a slice start aiming more left to compensate for it, or pull their right foot back to try to get the club swinging through more from the inside. These compensations pile up to the point where so many things have to happen to get the swing back on the right plane that it's luck if it happens at all.

Part of the problem is that the concept of swing plane is easy enough to understand, but it's difficult to see for yourself when you're actually over the ball. Unless you're watching yourself on video, it's hard to know what your swing plane is and what mistakes you're making.

A simple way to fix that situation is to set up a practice station with a couple of guide clubs—a drill I learned from my good friend Rob Akins. Put two clubs directly on the target line, one extending in front of the ball toward the target, with the butt end a foot in front of the ball, and the other extending away from the target, with the butt end a foot behind the ball.

This set of guide clubs serves two extremely valuable roles. First, it acts as a physical reminder of where you want the club shaft to be pointing throughout the swing. On the takeaway, the clubhead continues to point at spots moving down the rear guide shaft until the shaft of the club you're holding is parallel to the ground, and then the butt end points at the same line all the way to the top of the backswing. The same holds true but in opposite order on the downswing, and as the clubhead passes through impact, it continues to point down the lead guide shaft. You can even buy a laser device that screws into the bottom of your grip and throws a beam down on the guides, so you can measure how well you're doing. Second, the guides give you a great takeaway checkpoint.

The first three or four feet of the backswing set into motion a variety of motions and weight shifts that ultimately determine whether or not a shot will be struck cleanly. If you get out of sequence at the beginning, the rest of the swing will be a series of compensations and catch-ups. When you take the club back, you should be moving the clubhead the earliest and the most. In a good swing, that puts the shaft in your hands parallel to the rear guide club when is the shaft is waist high and parallel to the ground in your takeaway. It's very easy to make a few abbreviated practice swings back to just waist high and compare the position of your club with the guide club on the ground.

How the club behaves in this early part of the backswing tells you a lot about your sequencing issues. If you shift the grip instead of setting the wrists and letting the clubhead swing back, the club in your hands will point to the outside of the guide club. This is a precursor to a too-upright backswing plane. Lifting the arms and swinging back with no body turn will also cause the club in your hands to point to the outside of the guide club. If you over-rotate your forearms and pull the club inside, the club will point in front of the guide club. From this flat backswing plane you will have to come over the top to compensate.

What does good full-swing sequencing feel like in the backswing? It starts with an early set of the wrists, followed by the folding of the right elbow and the beginning of an upper-body turn. The resistance of the left arm against the torso signals the start of the upper-body turn, and the club travels up to a comfortable position at the top of the backswing.

On any shot from a putt to a full swing, yanking or pushing the club off the natural plane it wants to travel on will cause a host of sequencing and aiming issues. When I watch a player putt or hit a chip shot, my advice is often to get out of the way of the club and stop overcontrolling it. My full-swing advice is strikingly similar, with an accommodation for the fact that you have to generate a lot more clubhead speed.

In fact, it's the desire to create that downswing speed that causes so many problems in the full swing. Many players gear up to hit the ball hard by making a big upper-body turn to start the downswing. This move is a sequencing killer, and it wreaks havoc on both the tilt of the swing plane and the direction the plane is aimed. The big upper-body turn leaves the arms and the club behind, still at the top of the backswing, and it shifts the direction of the swing to the left. Now the arms have to catch up as they move down through impact, and the plane and the path are skewed to the left. This forces the player to try to throw the clubhead or hold it off to save the shot. The result? Slices, pushes, and pulls.

I deliver the same message for the downswing on a chip and a pitch as I do for the full swing. The swing starts from the ground up, and you need to lead with the lower body turning, let the arms and club start to fall down with no conscious effort, and then begin to unwind the upper body.

Working on creating a consistent swing plane in a small pitch shot is a great way to develop this sequencing and on-plane feel, because the bottom of a pitch-shot swing is identical to that of a full shot. The same things are happening, in the same order, just a little bit slower. A great way to improve your feel for this is to start by hitting soft half-pitches to a target 20 or 30 yards away, slowly increase the speed and size of your swing to a 50-yard shot, and then hit a full wedge—concentrating on the downswing sequencing of the lower body, with the arms dropping and the upper body turning, that we've discussed here.

A more sophisticated plane concept is one in which the clubface remains square to the path throughout the swing. It's easy to see and understand on a putt, and there are pictures of it in the color insert in the middle of this book. On a stroke that stays close to the ground, the club moves on a short arc. On a good stroke, the face of the putter appears to open on the backswing and close after impact. It is crucial to understand that you shouldn't be doing any twisting of the grip or fanning and shutting of the putterface to *make* the club open or shut. From your vantage point as the player looking down, when the club goes back from the ball, it moves inside the target line slightly,

To verify that your swing is staying on the right plane, construct a simple practice station with two clubs (1), both set on the target line. One club should extend about a foot behind the ball, with the butt end of the club pointing at the ball, and the other should extend toward the target with the butt end about a foot in front of the ball. As you make slow practice takeaways, keep the club in your hand pointed at the guide club on the ground behind the ball (2). The butt end of the club should point at the guide as you make your way to the top of the backswing (3).

When your backswing gets out of sequence, so does your swing plane. By shifting the grip back instead of setting the wrists and swinging the clubhead (4), the club points beyond the guide club. When you roll your forearms and pull the club inside (5), the club in your hands points to the inside.

The mistakes correspond on the downswing. On an over-the-top move (6), the butt of the club is pulled inside and points to the inside of the target line. When the right elbow gets trapped on the downswing from a slide and a tilt (7), the butt of the club points beyond the guide.

In an ideal finish, the club releases and heads up on the same plane line as at address (8). Extend a line from the butt of the club in my hand and it would point directly at the ball (9).

and the face opens in relation to the target. However, as long as you aren't manipulating your hands, the face is still square to the path.

That's fine for a stroke that operates in a three-foot arc, but what about in a full swing? You probably won't be surprised by what I'm going to tell you—and it will make your golf life easier. When the club is below your waist, both on the backswing and the through-swing, the face should stay square to the path, just as it does on a putt or a chip or a pitch. When the club is above the waist, the face should be at a 90-degree angle to the path. In golf terms, that's what's known as being "square" at the top of the backswing (or at any other point during the second half of the backswing).

Players get in trouble when they shift the grip end of the club and pull the swing plane either out of circle or off-kilter in terms of aim. When you manipulate the grip end in the backswing, it causes the clubface to stray from a position that's square to the path from below the waist and square to the target above the waist.

I don't want to go too far down the technical road, because the whole point of this book is to get you connected with sequence versus form. As I said before, really smart guys like my friend Jim Hardy have written multiple books about the various planes involved in the golf swing, and those books are a great place to go for a "masters class" on this subject. And the last thing I want you to do is to go out and freeze during different parts of your backswing to make sure that your club is exactly square to the path, or square to the target.

I'm giving you this information as a background explanation for why your short-game swing and full-shot swing are a lot more than just second cousins. They're brother and sister.

# Chapter 8

# DIAGNOSING YOUR BALL FLIGHT

. . . . . . . . . . . . . . . . . . . . . . . . . . . . . . . . . . . . . . . . . . .

To get a complete, comprehensive picture of what's happening during your golf swing, you obviously need to get in front of a teacher, a video camera, or a TrackMan machine, a radar device that measures the exact position of the club through the impact area of the swing. It's no different than having the transmission in your car checked out by a mechanic using all the latest diagnostic machines. But just because the mechanic has the definitive word on the problem in your car doesn't mean you don't notice when it just isn't running right.

The exact same thing is true in your golf swing.

To get better as a player, you need to be able to evaluate the way your ball flies (on shots) or rolls (on putts) and determine if it's doing what you want and expect it to. Even if you aren't sure how to fix a problem you see, being able to identify it gives you a place to start the next time you practice, or the next time you see a teacher.

My goal here is to actually take you one step further than that and show you how to understand some of the base causes for the ball flight you see. If you know the causes and are able to apply the sequencing ideas we've been talking about in this book to your particular problem, you can fix it at a time when it matters the most—out on the course. How many times have you played the first four or five holes of your round just awfully, making the same kinds of mistakes over and over again but having no idea how to get the ball going less crooked? Instead of giving in and accepting the idea that you're going to shoot 92, you'll have some tools to be able to pull yourself out of it.

Call it ball-flight ground work.

As I said in the beginning, it's no substitute for a full video session, lesson, or TrackMan appointment, but a sharper eye will be a big help.

Let's start with putting.

# PUTTING

If you come out to see me for a putting lesson at Grayhawk in Scottsdale, the first thing I'll ask you is about the putts that give you trouble. Do you miss the short ones or do you have trouble lagging it close from long range? Do you tend to pull putts or push them out to the right?

By asking those questions, I'm trying to get you to tell me what you think the solution is for your own problems. There are three possible ways you could answer. One, you correctly identify what your problem putt is, but you can't figure out how to consistently avoid it. Two, you identify an issue, but it doesn't match what I see when I watch you. Three, you don't know why you miss the putts you do.

Any of those three answers is a productive first step. If you understand why you're missing putts, you're one step closer to fixing the problem. You just need a piece of mechanical advice or a technical adjustment to get you going in the right direction.

If you're not identifying the right problem, getting some guidance from me on the real issues will remove a lot of frustration. You're going to have a "so *that's* what I'm doing" moment— and you'll probably feel like the solution isn't nearly as difficult as you thought. A great example of this is the student who comes in complaining about three-putting too much. He'll usually say it's because he doesn't make enough short putts. I'll take that guy out for nine holes to gauge what's going on, and I usually see the same thing. On a long putt—of, say, 30 feet— he'll yank the grip back and use a tremendous amount of effort to get the ball to the hole. He won't have much touch, and one ball will end up eight feet short and the next will go six feet past the hole. And when he misses the come-backer, he focuses on his short putting. But the real culprit is an inefficient putting stroke that is robbing him of any lag putting feel. Once we fix that problem, his distance control gets dialed-in and he's looking at a lot of three-footers instead of a six-footer. And if you don't think that's a big deal, just look at the stats from the PGA Tour. Tour players miss half their putts from six feet. Bump the ball up to three feet and they make almost 80 percent. Get just a little better on your lag putting and you can make a tremendous difference in your score.

Even if you don't know what kind of problem you have with your roll, that's good, too. As soon as you get a feel for good putt sequencing and develop a sound, efficient process, you're going to get way better.

Once you've deciphered what part of the putting game gives you the most trouble, it's time to investigate the stroke itself. I just spent a couple of days with an outstanding amateur player who consistently shot scores in the low 70s. He said putting was the best part of his game. I watched him for ten minutes on the practice green and saw that on a long putt, the grip moved 10 inches past the ball through impact. The way I teach, that grip should barely move at all. I was leery about changing too much in his swing, because he really knew how to get the ball in the hole. But we started out by making some exaggerated, wristy one-handed swings that forced him to stop moving the grip and let the putterhead swing. Then I had him exaggerate rolling the putterface open on the backswing and closed through the downswing. In the end, those feels helped him realize that he didn't need to shift his elbows out and away from his body during his putting stroke. The putterhead could pass his hands and that was all right. His stroke got much smaller—immediately—and more efficient. He was a good putter already—but streaky—and when he understood his misses, he got even better almost immediately. He had been getting the ball in the hole, but he knew he wasn't hitting it solid. When he improved his stroke, he stopped hitting putts thin and started hitting them square. His distance control got way better, and he started making a lot more of the 10- and 12-footers that can separate a good round from a great one.

If you tend to push putts out to the right, it's usually because you have a stroke path that comes from inside and continues across the target line. It often happens because you're trying to accelerate the grip toward the cup through impact, and this pushes the swing path to the outside. It's also often the result of a closed stance and closed shoulders at address. You can be a good putter from that address position, but you have to release the putterface consciously and aggressively with the hands and wrists to compensate for the non-neutral setup.

If you pull putts, it's usually happening because you've released the putterhead through impact, but the grip hangs back. Or, if you swing the putter and lead with the heel through impact, you might expect the open putterface to lead to pushes out to the right. But, ironically, the miss that comes from leading the heel is often a pull. I believe this happens because the brain knows the ball is about to start off-line to the right, and it corrects so that the player pulls across the ball with a left path. The overcompensation causes the ball to start left. If the player tries rotating the putterface early enough to get it back to square at impact (which in the beginning will seem to cause more of a left miss), he or she will find that the left miss quickly disappears.

Slicing and hooking putts happen the same way as they would in the full swing. When you slice a putt, you do it with an open putterface and a path that comes from the outside in. The ball might not show signs of a slice after the first two or three feet of roll, but I can tell you from experience that a putt hit with hook spin tends to roll a lot more smoothly than one hit with cut spin.

Speaking of hooking putts, those are caused by an in-to-out path and a closed putterface. As I said, hook spin causes the ball to roll very well. Bobby Locke—the South African who won four British Opens in the 1940s and 1950s—was probably the most famous hook putter of all time. I never saw him play, but my friend Gary McCord watched him in person, and he told me to find videos of Locke on YouTube. Locke was a completely wristy putter—he loaded the entire club with a wrist hinge, and threw it at the ball. The most common thing I hear about that style is that it wouldn't work on today's faster greens, but I don't get that at all. One of my good friends, Tom, came to seem me a couple of years ago at almost sixty years old. He was a 12-handicap and really interested in improving his game. In our first lesson together, I asked him all the questions we've discussed in this chapter. He said he used to be a great putter when he was young, but it left him. I asked him to show me what he used to do, and it was this gorgeous, wristy stroke. Basically, I got him to go back to what he had been doing as a young man, but with a longer putter because he's so tall. He had played all his life and gotten stiff from the "rules" of golf instruction. But he still had that old stroke in his DNA.

It's simple enough to recognize that the ball is coming off the face as a push or a pull, but what happens when you've got the yips? Nothing compares with the desperation I see in students who come to me believing that they've lost control of their hands that way. The problem is a big one—one that deserves its own book—but when it comes to reading the roll of a yipped putt, I have some advice. The yip itself comes from lifting the handle upward and opening the face at impact. You never see a player yip the ball by throwing the head and turning the face to the left. If this is a problem you have, you want to put yourself in a position where you have to hit down on the ball and close the face. Creating a change is the key to short-circuiting the yip.

## CHIPPING AND PITCHING

The vast majority of chipping and pitching problems turn up when a player opens his stance, aims left, and swings the handle hard toward the target. That setup is perfect if you're interested in hitting a push block—and you're good enough to clip the ball perfectly from the turf every time. I don't know why you would actually try to hit a shot less than solid, but that's what that setup promotes. Problems with thin and fat shots happen when the player shifts the bottom of his swing arc too far behind the ball. This same mistake of having the swing bottom out too soon usually happens when the player tries to lift the ball into the air. I believe that establishing your pivot point at address and keeping it through the swing simplifies things dramatically.

Assuming you use the setup and sequencing we've talked about in this book, you should be able to reduce the spectrum of possible mistakes. But there's still pushing and pulling shots, and hitting them too low or too high.

When you pull a pitch or a chip, it's usually because the pivot in your swing happens in the back foot instead of the front one. The upper body then over-rotates on the way through impact and the swing path goes dramatically to the left. The key to sorting out a pull is to start at address with more of your weight shifted to your front foot, and to make that front foot the axis of your pivot.

A pushed shot is a result of the opposite mix of characteristics. In this case, the body shifts toward the target instead of pivoting, the grip moves forward past the ball, and the clubface hangs open. The fix is the same one that works with a pull—start with your weight primarily on the front foot and keep it there while pivoting from that axis. Then just let the club release naturally.

We've talked about controlling the height of chips and pitches intentionally through the position of the left wrist through impact, but here I want to focus on problem shots that go too low or too high because of a mechanical or sequencing problem. If you're struggling to get your chip shots in the air, it's most likely happening because you're dragging the grip through impact ahead of the clubhead and keeping the leading edge of the face, instead of the bottom of the bounce, exposed to the ground. This is often a result of using a super-strong grip and turning the clubface closed on the backswing. In essence, you're turning your 56-degree wedge into a 7-iron. Without a grip overhaul, it will always be very hard to hit a high shot from this setup.

If a player hits high, weak shots, it's usually because he doesn't trust the loft of the club to provide enough height, so he hangs his weight on his back foot and tries to scoop the ball in the air. This kind of swing—with no body turn or pivot—doesn't generate any pressure on the ball. It's that pressure from the club hitting the ball and then the turf with its true loft that pops a shot into the air.

# FULL SWING

My friends Jim Hardy and Mike Adams have literally written books on diagnosing ball-flight problems, so I won't go into a lengthy description of the dozens of variations you might see. But I think it's important to talk about a few common ball-flight problems that you'll encounter, just to give you some security.

The most common "bad" ball flights I see are the high and weak shot to the right, the over-the-top pull, and the no-clubhead-speed powder-puff shot. Many, many golfers fall into one of those three categories—and there are some relatively simple fixes.

If you can't understand why your 7-iron is only going 115 yards into the right rough, you have to look at the clubface. Tour players get to impact having turned the 7-iron in their hand into the effective loft of a 5-iron. They're compressing the ball. Players who hit high, weak shots to the right are doing the opposite—they're adding loft. Instead of hitting a 7-iron, they're turning the 7-iron into a 9-iron by leaning the shaft backward through impact, coupled with an open clubface.

The most common reason for this problem is, believe it or not, effort. When a player sees those shots going weak and right, he usually aims more to the left and tries to swing harder.

But "harder" usually translates into pulling the left shoulder down toward the ball too early in the downswing and pivoting off the back foot. The player falls back and spins the body too early, which moves the bottom of the swing to the right—away from the ball. With the stance aimed to the left, it just produces shots that go even higher and farther to the right.

The solution to the weak-and-rights is to locate the bottom of the swing in the right place and let the swing unwind in the right order. Instead of aiming more left—which, in effect, is opening the stance—keep your aim square to the target and make a full shoulder turn on the backswing. Then, from the top, let the hands and clubhead fall toward the ground first, just through gravity, before starting the unwinding of the upper body. By making a more controlled, sequenced downswing, you're going to stop yourself from lunging at the ball. Making more consistent contact with the ball at the bottom of your swing arc will be an almost immediate positive benefit.

The player who comes over the top and hits a low-left screamer is often doing so because he's got a strong grip and he's rolling his forearms hard through impact. If you're that guy, the first thing you need to realize is that when you set your grip at address, if your hands come back through impact rolled more toward the target than when you started, the clubface is shut. The ball will go hard left unless you rotate your body really fast to keep the clubface from flipping over too soon. David Duval and Paul Azinger won a lot of money doing it that way—using aggressive body pivot and little to no forearm rotation.

My own problem shot has always been the low-left one. The truth is, my actual swing problem should have caused a bad miss to the right. I was just good enough as an athlete that when the right miss was about to happen, I would reflexively overcompensate for it as I tried to make a correction, and there was my bad hook. I'd stop my body from turning through and try to time my wrists to get the clubhead back to square. If my timing was good, I'd have a good day. But when I was off, I'd hit nasty flip hooks or—after I knew what was coming—big blocks to the right when my brain was trying to save me from my hands.

Players with the last problem—no distance and clubs that all go the same yardage—are the most fun to fix. I see it most often in older players—guys who swing the club on a good plane but never really unleash the clubhead. These players have slowly lost the wrist action in their swing, and even though they're moving the arms at the same speed they did five years earlier, they wonder where those 20 yards went. If you learn (or relearn) how the wrists should hinge on a full shot—up and down like cracking a whip, not rolling over like you're waving a protest sign—you can refire the best speed generator in your swing and get that yardage back.

# Chapter 9

# YOUR 30-DAY PRACTICE PLAN

· · · · · · · · · · · · · · · · · · · · · · · · · · · · · · · · · · · · · · · · · · · · · · · · · ·

Now that you've made your way through these chapters, you might be wondering how long it will take to see real improvement in your swing sequencing—whether it's in your putting, short game, full swing, or all of the above. I can tell you that I've had students come to see me in Scottsdale in the morning, and by lunchtime, the sensation of the clubhead swinging with speed has clicked with them.

Does that mean you're going to be able to walk onto the golf course a half hour after reading this book and have all the concepts locked down? Not exactly. Even after you start feeling the speed on the business end of the club, it still takes some time to have confidence in the technique and a sense for what the ball will do with your newfound clubhead speed. You'll probably start out by hitting putts and chips a little longer than you expect, and you'll have to recalibrate the distances in your irons to account for the extra length you'll be getting. Not the worst problems to have, but factors you have to consider.

If you've read any of my other books, you know I believe

that every player has the ability to pick up these concepts and play a more athletic game. When it comes to sequencing your swing, I believe that if you dedicate a month of thirty-minute practice sessions made up of equal parts putting, short game and full swing, you can make a significant change in your game—and your handicap—in those 30 days. Does that mean you need to go hard for 30 days in a row? The plan isn't physically demanding, so you could certainly do it if you had the time. But you'll get just as much from it if you do it two or three times a week over a few months.

We're going to go over that 30-day plan in detail here, but first, I want to say a few words about the importance of having equipment that fits you. You need to go into this process with the best chance of success, and an equipment assessment is one of the first things I do when I get a new student.

Let's start with putters. The three basic measurements you need to know are all L's—length, lie angle, and loft. The length and lie angle work together to match your body and stroke. If you're a tall person, you obviously need a longer putter—but it isn't as easy as getting a 36-inch shaft instead of a 34-inch one. You also need the lie angle of the club—the angle at which the shaft comes out of the head—to suit your body and your stroke. If the lie angle of the putter is too upright, you'll stand very close to the ball with the putter flat on the ground and make a stroke that doesn't arc very much. Standard putters come with about 71 degrees of lie angle. When I fit you, you'll probably end up with one a little flatter, which promotes more of an arcing stroke.

Getting set up by a perceptive clubfitter is important, but I can give you an idea of whether or not your putter is in the ballpark. When you're in a comfortable setup position and your elbows are slightly bent at your sides, your putter needs to reach the ground and rest flat on the grass. Most players have putters that are too short and too upright. If they set up the way I just described, the toe of the putter would be off the ground.

Loft is the third piece of the putter-fitting puzzle, and it has a lot to do with the quality of roll you get off the face. You might think a putter wouldn't need any loft. After all, you're hitting the ball along the ground, not launching it. But even on the super-short grass of the putting green, the ball sits down in the blades of grass slightly when you're at address. To propel the ball out of that little depression and get it rolling smoothly, you need to have some loft on the putter. Many of them come from the factory with 2 or 3 degrees of loft. I like to see players use a slight forward press at the beginning of the swing, which reduces the effective loft of the putter, so I like to have 4 or 5 degrees of loft on the putter.

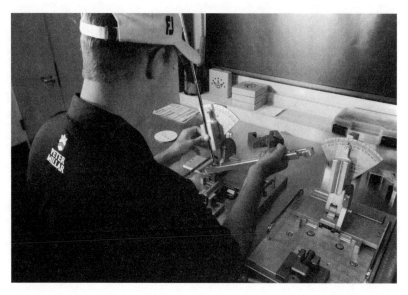

I use a Scotty Cameron lie-loft machine to check the specifications of each putter my students bring. It measures the lie angle of the putter—the angle created by the shaft and the sole of the club—and the loft on the face in degrees. Most times, I can bend the putter to adjust it to better fit the student, but occasionally I need to replace a shaft—or they need to get an entirely different style head.

The kind of head you pick for your putter is a matter of preference. If you like a lot of aiming aids and graphics, that's fine and great, and up to you. You do have to pay attention to the way the head is weighted, though, and to make sure that the weighting matches your stroke. Putterheads are either "face-balanced" or built with different degrees of "toe hang." If you balance the club on your finger, a face-balanced putter will balance with the face pointing to the sky. That kind of putter promotes a stroke that moves on a straight-back-and-through path—the opposite of what I teach. I like putters that are built with more weight toward the toe—this makes the toe angle toward the ground (thus the term "toe hang") when you balance the club on your finger. Toe hang helps the club swing around in an arc.

**At the Titleist Performance Institute in Oceanside, California, Dave Phillips (right) uses a variety of cutting edge tools to measure a player's putting stroke both for clubfitting and for instruction. Here, he's using a system of cameras to measure the path of my putting stroke, the location of the clubhead in space through impact, and the quality of roll the stroke produces on the ball. With all of that data, he can both put a player in a putter that will produce a better, more consistent roll and also see any aim or stroke flaws that need to be fixed.**

Length and lie angle are just as important through the rest of your set, both irons and woods, as shaft flex. When you get a dynamic fitting from a clubfitter, he or she can set up the clubs so that they help correct your predominant flaw. Irons that are built more upright encourage more of a right-to-left curve, while clubs that are built flatter produce a more left-to-right curve. It's extremely important to remember that your wedges need to be fit separately from your irons. While it might be great to have a 6-iron that's built upright to prevent you from slicing, you need to have wedges with a more neutral lie angle so that you have the flexibility to hit a variety of shots around the green.

Using the right flex will help you produce the best ball flight for your strength level. If you use shafts that are too stiff, you won't be able to get the shaft to load and unload, and you'll give up lots of swing speed and height on your shots. If you use shafts that are too soft, you'll produce too much load on the shaft and it will torque uncontrollably through impact.

One underrated component in the iron- and driver-fitting process is the grip. Many players hold the club in the wrong place—across the palm—when they're measuring themselves for new grips. As a result, they get grips that are too big for their hands, and it restricts the hinging and unhinging of the wrists and the release of the club through impact. You need to get grips that fit when the handle is down in the fingers.

When it comes to fitting a driver, head shape is a matter of preference, just as it is with the putter. Shaft technology and fitting play a huge part in finding success with the longest club in the bag, and I think it's a big mistake to buy a driver without getting fit on a launch monitor. You need to be able to see how different shaft and loft combinations impact your spin rate. A good-fitting driver should produce about 3,000 rpm of back-spin. If you manage to get that right off the rack, it's really just pure luck. Good clubfitters have dozens of different shafts and four or five different lofts in a clubhead to get you the most mileage out of your club. Let them help.

Set makeup is the last piece of the fitting puzzle. You can carry fourteen clubs, and it's obviously best to get the most out of them. A standard set has a driver, 3-wood, 5-wood, 3- to 9-irons, three wedges, and a putter. If your handicap is higher than 10, I believe you need to get rid of your 3- and 4-irons and replace them with hybrids. Many tour players have done this with at least their 3-iron. If it's good enough for them, it's good enough for you.

How far you hit your clubs (or what the numbers say on the bottom) really doesn't matter. What matters is that you have regular intervals between the comfortable range of distances you hit each club. If you can hit your 9-iron between 125 and 130 yards, it makes sense to have an 8-iron that you can hit between 130 and 135, and so on. If you move through the set to the longer clubs and end up with a big gap—say, from your 5-iron to your first hybrid—you run the risk of facing a shot out on the course and not having the right club for it.

For wedges, it's important to have the right mix of lofts and bounce angles to suit the conditions and kinds of shots you like to play. Sand wedges come with everything from no bounce to 10 or 12 degrees, and the amount of bounce directly correlates to whether or not the club skips through grass or sand or if the leading edge digs into the ground. The higher the bounce number on the club, the more it will skip instead of dig.

I think you can hit a majority of your short-game shots with a good all-purpose wedge—58 degrees of loft and 10 degrees of bounce. Then you can fill in with a 48-degree pitching wedge and a 52-degree gap wedge for longer shots from the fairway. If you have trouble hitting super-high shots around the green, you could change the 58-degree club to a 56 and also carry a 60-degree wedge.

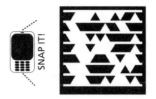

Depending on the kind of player you are, you can modify your set to give yourself more choices on long shots or short ones. If you have a lot of clubhead speed, you can probably get away with one less fairway wood or hybrid and get a benefit from using an extra wedge. Slower swingers need more options from long distance, so the third wedge could come out in favor of another fairway wood.

Once you have your set put together, you're ready to get to work on the 30-day plan. I've designed it so that you can do the entire circuit in thirty minutes, but that doesn't mean you have to limit yourself to that if you have more time to practice. You'll get a positive multiplier effect if you stack more than one set of these drills in the specific game area you're trying to improve. But even if you just follow the basic plan I outline below, you'll see some dramatic changes.

## PUTTING CIRCUIT: TEN MINUTES

Start with a series of a dozen 30- to 50-foot putts, hitting three or four balls in rapid succession using only the right hand. Switch to left-hand-only for another dozen putts, and then do a series with both hands, hitting them freely and rapidly and letting the clubhead swing. At this point, you're only paying attention to how the ball comes off the face. You're looking for contact in the center of the face, and for the ball rolling, not bouncing. After five minutes, take three balls and practice some putts from nine feet. But instead of just mindlessly rattling off putt after putt, work on the routine we talked about in Chapter 4, from lining up the logo on your ball to the target line to walking in and taking your stance. The goal is to ingrain the same pre-putt routine for every putt you hit, whether it's on the practice green or the course. That helps to put the focus on the routine rather than the stakes when it comes to a pressure situation on-course. Finish off the session with a few makes from 18-inches or so.

## SHORT-GAME CIRCUIT: TEN MINUTES

For this circuit, you need to get yourself one of those simple, cheap shag tubes they sell at any golf discount store. The tube has a plastic insert in the bottom that lets you walk around and click up your practice balls quickly, making your practice time much more efficient—and the practice green a lot cleaner for you and your fellow players. The tube slides right into your bag, and it usually holds about twenty-four balls. It's good to have that many practice balls of the same kind that you usually use on the course, for consistency.

Start your circuit with low chip-and-run shots with either a 54- or a 58-degree wedge, and concentrate on your footwork and your pivot. Turn into a straight left leg, with your right heel releasing off the ground and your right knee turning in toward your left knee—not out toward the ball. Remember, this shot has very little grip swing. The clubhead moves the most, and you're turning your left forearm down on the way through impact to produce the low shot.

After five minutes, move to a standard pitch shot in which you carry five steps of fringe to a hole no more than 25 feet away. The goal here is to produce a shot that lands softly and doesn't roll very far. Hinge the wrists on your takeaway and rotate the right forearm to open the face and add a little bit of loft, then work on releasing the clubhead back through impact without rolling the forearms, which would reduce the loft and the bounce on the club. If you have trouble with this feel, hit some shots with just the right hand and finish with your right palm facing up—which keeps the bounce exposed to the ground through impact. You can take this exact same pitch setup and practice routine and move to the bunker if you have a few extra minutes—the technique for exposing the bounce and getting the club to skip through the sand is the same.

## FULL-SWING CIRCUIT: TEN MINUTES

One drill that I've used with a lot of success to help students get a feel for good sequencing and speed on the clubhead end is to simply swing two feet over the ball and take golf out of the mix. It comes from a tip I got from Dave Musgrove—a world-class caddie who carried for Seve Ballesteros, Sandy Lyle, Lee Janzen, and Ian Woosnam. He was supposed to be on Scott Hoch's bag one week and Scott withdrew, and I was short a caddie so I hired Dave. As the week went along and he saw me fussing around with my stance and my backswing and a bunch of other mechanical thoughts, he said something I've never forgotten: "Just swing the clubhead and it will tell everything else where to go." In other words, if you can let the clubhead go fast, it's your best guide. Make two or three of those swings two or three feet above the ball, almost like a baseball swing, and then without stopping to adjust your stance or think about mechanics, bend over and hit the shot. You don't have time to freeze over the ball or get paralyzed with mechanical analysis. You're getting out of the way of your athleticism. Repeat this sequence for about five minutes and you'll be amazed at how much more freely you can swing the clubhead.

For the second half of the circuit, start with an 8-iron, making a slow, three-quarter arm swing. Turn into the backswing, release the arms down toward the ball and then turn through the shot. You're trying to keep your body from racing out in front of the clubhead and your arms. Once you feel this natural unwinding and clubhead speed—to a balanced finish on a tall left leg and with your belt buckle facing the target—move up to a hybrid club and go through the same process. To finish, do the same drill using five balls with your driver—focusing on letting the arms drop first from the top and the body turning after. If you can't hold your finish with your weight fully on your left foot, your left leg straight and tall, and your belt buckle facing your target, you need to slow the process down and hit softer shots until you can work your way back to full speed.

# Chapter 10

# SEQUENCING QUICK REFERENCE GUIDE

. . . . . . . . . . . . . . . . . . . . . . . . . . . . . . . . . . . . . . . . . . . .

U nderstanding the sequence of motion in the variety of golf shots—a putt versus a pitch versus a bunker shot versus a full swing—gives you a fantastic toolbox to take with you when you play. It's good to know basic setup mechanics, but when shots start going sideways, it's usually a sequencing issue that's to blame. Think of it as changing your process from controlling what your body does during a swing to making the clubhead swing. That one basic idea will help you on any shot from a two-footer for par to a 200-yard forced carry off the tee of a long par-5.

Below are some of the key points from the previous nine chapters, summarized so you can brush up or go back and find the full explanation you need.

# Form vs. Sequence

■ "Form" in a golf swing is how your body and club positions compare with those of an ideal swing. It's the basic mechanics of how you set up and hold the club and the technical accuracy of your swing moment by moment.

■ "Sequence" is the dynamic measure of how the elements of a swing work together to produce an efficient shot. Players can have weak form and excellent sequencing, and vice versa.

■ To play consistent golf, you need to understand the right form elements for different shots, as well as the proper sequencing of body and clubhead needed to execute them.

■ A good putting grip is designed to keep touch and feel in the fingertips and keep your hands in a neutral position through the stroke. Hold the putter up in front of you with your right hand positioned on the shaft just under the grip and with the face vertical to the ground. Now squeeze your left thumb down toward the palm of your hand. Place your thumb down the top of your putter grip so that it presses firmly against the lifeline. I would rather you make a mistake with your left hand turned a little more to the right than the left. Place the right hand so that the lifeline connects with the last knuckle of your middle finger. The fingertips are the main contact points on the grip.

■ A good putting setup position is neutral, with the feet, hips, and shoulders parallel to the target line and neither forearm set higher or lower than the other.

■ On a full swing, the grip is designed to promote the hinging and unhinging of the wrists. Instead of running up the lifelines and in line with the forearm as in a putting grip, the full-swing grip sets the club down in the fingers, along the creases created by the lowest segment of each finger.

■ The most common full-swing grip types are overlapping and interlocking. In the overlapping grip, the pinky finger of the right hand rests on top of the left hand, between the knuckles of the index and middle fingers. In the interlocking, the pinky finger on the right hand links with the left index finger.

■ If you set your grip in front of you and hold your hands up in front of your chest, the V's created by the sides of your hands and thumbs will point toward your right ear in a perfectly neutral grip. In a "strong" grip, your hands are turned on the grip so that the V's are pointed toward your right shoulder. In a "weak" grip, the hands are turned the opposite way, so the V's point to your chin. The relative strength or weakness of your grip determines how easy or hard it is to rotate your forearms and release the club through impact. With a strong grip, the forearms rotate very little through impact, while the opposite is true of a weak grip.

## Moving Energy to the Clubhead

■ The movement in a swing can be broken down into three circles. The body moves in the first, smallest circle, in the form of the hip and shoulder turn. The hands and grip move in the second circle—which is a little bigger than the first one because it's happening at the end of the arms. The biggest circle is the one being traced by the clubhead.

■ To hit effective golf shots, a player must sequence the rotation of the three circles so that they reach the ball in the appropriate order.

■ The wrists provide energy and snap on the clubhead through impact. The wrists can move in several different ways, depending on the shot required—back and forth (as in a putting stroke), up and down (as in a full shot), and back and under (as in a bunker shot).

■ One of the most common ways that a player can transfer energy to the wrong end of the club is to shift the grip back in the backswing, rather than hinging the wrists and letting the clubhead swing.

■ Practice hitting long putts with just the right hand to get the feel of loading and unloading the clubhead using wrist action. It will be impossible to hit the putts if you shift the grip back and forth.

## Controlling the Clubface

■ With a neutral grip, the back of the left wrist represents the face of the club. Controlling the loft on a shot involves changing the relationship between the back of the left wrist and the ground through impact.

■ By turning the back of the left wrist down toward the ball through impact, you reduce the effective loft on the clubface and produce lower shots. By holding the back of the left wrist angled upward, you increase the effective loft and produce a higher shot.

■ Making slow, left-handed practice swings with a Ping-Pong paddle reinforces the connection between the back of the wrist and the face. Practice swinging through with the face of the paddle turned down and turned upward.

■ You can use hook spin and slice spin on chips and pitches to tailor the shot to your situation. Hooked shots roll out more, while sliced shots fly higher and land softer.

## Sequencing Your Game

■ Your pre-round routine should be designed to help you warm up and visualize the shots you'll actually be hitting out on the course. It isn't the time to experiment with different instruction tips or to pound balls mindlessly.

■ I get ready for a round by starting with some short pitch shots. I'm just trying to get the feel in my hands and arms and stretch out a little. I work my way through the bag for twenty to thirty minutes before ending with the club I'm going to hit off the first tee. I hit six or seven balls with that club—usually the driver or a 3-wood—then go to the practice bunker and spend five or ten minutes getting a feel for the sand conditions. When I have fifteen minutes to go before my tee time, I go to the practice green and hit a variety of 20-footers first, to help dial in my feel for distance. Then I finish up with a series of short 18-inch putts to reinforce the feeling of success—the ball going in the hole.

■ When you're playing a course for the first time, you can read a green with your eyes before you get there and then with your feet once you walk onto the putting surface. Watch your approach shot and see how the ball behaves. As you walk onto the green, note the prevailing tilt of the green—the low point will usually have drains for water runoff.

■ To read a putt, first look for the break from behind your ball, then walk behind the hole and look for it from that direction.

When you return to your ball from behind the hole, make sure to walk to the ball on the low side—opposite from the direction the ball will break—and look at the putt from a spot halfway to the hole. If the putt breaks from left to right, you want to walk to the right side of the hole and read the putt from halfway. From those three spots you can gain the most useful information about what the putt actually does.

■ Once you've determined the apex of the putt, your pre-shot routine should be geared toward lining yourself up to this point—not to the hole. Walk up to the ball with the putter in your right hand. Stand so your feet are perpendicular to your start line and turn your head to look where you want the ball to start, then set the putterhead behind the ball. I believe this is the most reliable way to aim the putter. Once the putter is in place, use the clubhead as the reference point to get settled into your putting stance.

■ If you can standardize your pre-shot routine, you can use it as your focus point and distract yourself from your nerves and your worry about what's going to happen if you miss.

■ On any short-game or full shot, visualize the complete ball flight from the time the ball leaves the club to where it lands and how far it rolls out. The more variables you plug into your calculation—wind, elevation change, firmness of the green, most dangerous places to miss—the more accurate your visualization will be, and the more likely your shot will be successful.

## Feels

■ A feel is a swing thought or impression that you plug in to help yourself focus on an important part of the swing movement. To find a feel that works for you, it has to connect with what you're trying to do, and it can't be overwhelmed by a dozen other mechanical and swing thoughts. When I play, I pick a swing thought that is working for me that day and focus on that thought alone during my pre-shot routine.

■ The kinds of feels that work for you will depend on the way you process information. If you're a visual person, it might be based on something you've seen a teacher or player do, or something you've seen yourself do on video when you're swinging well. If you're a more technical person, you might respond to a description. You might be a physical learner who responds when a teacher actually puts the club in a certain position—your feel is connected to re-creating that sensation.

■ Feels tend to be fleeting. What works for a round or for a week might not work the next round or the following week. The key is to build a library of feels that have worked for you, then page through your library before a given round and apply one that connects that day.

■ Reinforce positive feels and swing thoughts by taking an inventory of your good shots after every round. Mark on your scorecard the good shots you hit and what your swing thought was during those shots. Those cards can become a great reference tool.

## Five Shots You Can Play with One Club

■ Many teachers advocate changing clubs for different shots around the green. I believe you're a better player if you focus on one club—a 58-degree wedge—and develop different shots with it. With more repetitions, you come to know the one club much better than you would a variety of different clubs you hit infrequently.

■ By modifying your setup and downswing sequencing, you can easily hit five distinct shots with the same club—a low chip-and-run, a lofted pitch, a distance pitch, a bunker shot, and a trouble shot.

■ For a low-running chip, set up with your spine tilted left and your weight more on your front foot. Hinge the wrists on the backswing, let the club fall down to the ball through impact, and pivot around your left leg. Avoid making a large arm swing, which will force you to have to slow the club down through impact.

■ For a lofted pitch, you're adding more release with the hands through impact than you would for the low-running chip, so that the bounce of the club is exposed to the ground. Compared with the chip, you move two or three inches farther away from the ball at address, which adds loft to the club. Through impact it should feel as though your right palm is facing upward.

■ For a distance pitch, you're in the intermediate zone between a full swing and a lofted pitch. The key is to connect the distance of this shot with the size and speed of your lower-body pivot. Turn more and faster to hit a longer shot versus swinging your arms more and faster. Similar to the low chip and the lofted pitch, the ball is played from the center of the stance, and from a square to slightly closed stance.

■ Bunker shots and trouble shots use the same fundamentals— a vertical or slightly backward leaning shaft and hands set lower by virtue of being a few inches farther from the ball at address, but with a much wider stance. Your feet should be set wider than they would be for even a driver, with the same forward spine tilt that you would use for a low chip. Your ball position is slightly ahead of center and the clubface is slightly open. To swing, remember to make a hip turn during the backswing, hinge the wrists and lift the club, and then release it aggressively at the sand much earlier in the downswing than you would for the other shots. Finish forward and tall on the left side.

## The Full Swing

■ The phrase "plane" is very common in golf instruction. It can refer to the plane the shoulders are on, the arms are on, or the one created by the shaft at address. The goal here is to establish the right club-shaft plane for you at address and to make an efficient swing that stays on that plane throughout.

■ Problems arise when a player shifts or twists the club off the circular swing-plane path. This happens when the player pulls or shifts the handle instead of swinging the clubhead on the backswing, over-rotates the forearms, or unwinds the body and clubhead in the wrong sequence on the downswing.

■ To determine your best swing plane, make some swings with the club belt high, turning your hips and shoulders fully and moving the clubhead as fast as possible. Once you've reached full speed, bend over until the club brushes the ground and continue to make swings. The speed of the club moving through space will cause it to find an efficient circle.

■ To track the integrity of your swing plane, place the guide clubs on the ground—one in front of the ball along the target line starting a foot in front of the ball, and one behind the ball on the target line a foot from the ball. When the club in your hand is below your waist during the swing, the clubhead should point at the guide club behind the ball on the backswing and the guide club in front on the through-swing. When the club is above the waist, the butt end should point at the same lines in the backswing and through-swing.

## Diagnosing Ball Flight

■ To correct a ball-flight problem, you need to recognize what the problem is and apply the right solution. Many players don't know why they hit the shots they do, or they see the poor shots but don't know how to fix them.

■ On putts, if you hit pushes, it's usually because you have a stroke path that comes from inside and continues across the target line because the grip is accelerating toward the hole at impact. Pulled putts come from releasing the putter through impact but hanging the grip back.

■ Most chipping and pitching errors start with setup mistakes. If you play these shots from an open stance with the ball back in your stance, you have to chop down on the ball to hit it successfully.

■ Fat and thin chips usually happen because the player has moved the bottom of the swing arc back behind the ball, often by tilting the shoulders back in an effort to scoop the ball into the air or by failing to keep the weight on the front foot.

■ The most common full-swing ball-flight errors are the weak slice, the over-the-top pull and the no-speed short shot. The weak slice is caused by pulling the left shoulder hard at the ball from the top of the backswing and releasing the club too early, which adds loft. The over-the-top miss comes from using a grip that's too strong and over-rotating the forearms on the downswing. The weak shot comes from having wrists that aren't fully hinged in the backswing.

## 30-Day Practice Plan

■ The right array of equipment, properly fitted, is a good place to start. Clubs with the right length, lie, and shaft flex make it easier to hit the shots we've described. I advocate a set that includes a driver, a 3-wood, a 5-wood, hybrids replacing the two longest irons, the 5- through 9-irons, three wedges—a 48-degree pitching wedge, a 52-degree gap wedge, and a 58-degree sand wedge—and a putter.

■ You can accomplish all the things we've talked about in this book by following a thirty-minute practice routine consisting of ten-minute putting, short-game, and full-swing circuits.

■ In putting, start with a series of long right-hand-only putts, then hit long left-hand-only putts. Then work on nine-foot putts, hitting each one using your entire pre-putt routine, from read to stroke.

■ In the short game, start with low chips and move on to lofted pitches, hitting some low one-hand chips with the left hand and some high one-hand pitches with the right hand. Move to the bunker and use the pitch routine—one-handed shots—mixed with conventional practice.

■ For the full swing, start by making swings two or three feet over the ball with a wedge, building speed. Then bend over and immediately hit a ball. After several rounds of this, take an 8-iron and start with slow three-quarter shots, concentrating on your pivot. Move to a middle iron, hybrid, and then driver, repeating the process with each club.

# ACKNOWLEDGMENTS

I owe the inspiration for *The Art of the Swing* to one of my favorite students—my daughter, Tatum. She's always been extremely coachable and fun to hang out with, and it was during one of those hang-out times that I first used the words "form" and "sequence." My experience with her helped me define how I go about helping people with their golf games—and provided the foundation for the ideas you've read about here.

I also want to thank two fantastic teachers, Jim Hardy and Mike Adams, for continuing to encourage me as a teacher, and for supporting the idea that the way I teach people to putt and chip the ball—by releasing the clubhead, versus holding the angle—has an application beyond the short game. Jim in particular has been a mentor of mine ever since I dedicated myself to teaching six years ago.

The concepts for *The Art of the Swing* were there, but my friend Matt Rudy turned it into what you're holding in your hand. We wrote my previous three books—*The Art of Putting,*

*The Art of the Short Game*, and *The Art of Scoring*—together, and the process is always enjoyable. Matt came up with the plan to add the Microsoft Tag component to the project, making the video that so many of my students and fans have been asking for since the first book came out in 2006 accessible. J.D. Cuban did his usual fantastic job on the photographs for the book, and Ryan Noll did great work shooting and producing the video clips. My good friend and playing professional Tom Kalinowski was a valuable set of eyes on the photo shoot. Thanks also to Titleist and the team at TPI for providing us with a beautiful place to shoot pictures and video. On the business side, Scott Waxman and Farley Chase helped me continue my great relationship with Gotham, where the book was in the capable hands of Jessica Sindler.

My dad, Frank Utley, was my first coach, and I owe him and my mom, Ruby, special thanks for their positive influence. My brother John has been a best friend forever and is now the ultimate business associate. I've had a lot of great teachers over the years—from Ken Lanning back when I was a kid to Jim Parkins, Rich Poe, and Brian Allen during my college years. Craig Harrison, Fred Griffin, and Rob Akins have also helped a lot along the way. I learned a lot of what I teach from my fellow players out on tour—guys like Tom Pernice, Dillard Pruitt, Fred Wadsworth, and Brandel Chamblee are lifelong friends from whom I've learned a lot both inside and outside the ropes.

I have to thank my wife, Elayna, more than anyone. She's been my partner, my wife, my coach, and my best friend. I certainly couldn't have had the career I've had without her help. Tatum and my son, Jake, have both been a tremendous inspiration for me—as a teacher, a father, and a person.

I also want to acknowledge my Lord and Savior—the giver of great gifts, who has given me the passion to encourage others not just to know Him, but know and understand golf a little bit better.